FALL UP!

FALL UP!

TURN ADVERSITY INTO
YOUR SUPER-POWER

GREGG M. STEINBERG PHD

PEOPLE SHINE PUBLISHING

Nashville, Tennessee

WHAT PEOPLE ARE SAYING ABOUT *FALL UP!*

"Losing my eyesight totally and permanently in a car crash at age eighteen, I feared my life would be filled with an inability to make and keep relationships. But instead, I became a much more empathetic and understanding person. *Fall Up!* will teach you to harness the power of your own adversities and see your life in a wonderful new way!"

— **David Meador,** two-time national blind golf champion

"An unexpected terminal illness turned tragedy into inspiration and hope, redirecting my purpose in life. What I love about *Fall Up!* is that it helps you to find your purpose with effective, simple strategies."

— **Dr. Sandra F. Mulhinch,** clinical psychologist

"The tragic loss of my sister forced me to reevaluate my life and move into a new life purpose. *Fall Up!* shows everyone the process of what I went through as well as how you can transform your life into something wonderful."

— **Stephen Garrett,** M.S., grief counselor

"*Fall Up!* catches the essence of how tragedy can be reexamined and reshaped into a gift in your life."

— **Jim Stevens,** the Scrimshaw Studio

"A near-death experience became my wake-up call to living a life that really felt purposeful. I am hoping that *Fall Up!* will be your wake-up to help you discover your purpose in life."

— **Sam Russell,** founder of the Giving Closet

"*Fall Up!* is an incredibly inspiring book. The stories interwoven throughout are perfect examples of the principles of 'transcendability.'"

— **Kristin Willocks,** EdS, NCSP, school psychologist

"*Fall Up!* shows how you can turn your adversity into a tsunami of positive change."

— **Kia Scherr,** founder of One Life Alliance

ISBN: 978-0-578-80393-7

Cover design by 360 Media Group
Page layout by Win-Win Words LLC

Printed in the United States of America

To Tommie and Myles

CONTENTS

PROLOGUE

WHY THEY REALLY LEAN IN

"WHAT IS THE MASTER EMOTION?"

This is the opening question I ask when I start my seminars on emotional toughness. I am really trying to bring insight to which emotion leads to other powerful, positive emotions such as courage, grit, determination, confidence, and peace of mind.

Before I give the audience the answer (and now you), I share with them the essence of *Fall Up!* It all started a few years ago. I was sitting at a Starbucks with a friend, Joel Bunkowske, when we started discussing—for what became many hours—the concept of how people turn tragedy into transcendence, which I call transcend-ability. While Joel had experienced it firsthand (as you will find out later in the book), I also had a few friends who told me about their own amazing life transformations because of a hardship. Joel and I thought it was interesting that while there is some research on this topic, there are many questions still left unanswered.

To fill this gap as well as advance this idea, I interviewed people who said they had experienced transcendence from tragedy. Each person I interviewed shared how they had gone through specific stages, but ultimately their tragedy did not beat them down. Rather, their life difficulty helped them find their authentic self and achieve a life full of purpose on a daily basis—which is the essence of the process of transcend-ability and "falling up."

I am not exactly sure why transcend-ability happens. Perhaps tragedy is the darkness that allows you to see the light in your life. Maybe this pain gives perspective and provides a needed wake-up call to reevaluate your current position in life. Or, it could be the tragedy quiets all the noise and chaos in your life, allowing you to hear your "Lifesong." What I do know is that such a terrible moment or event helps to recreate in you a life filled with purpose.

So back to the initial question. What is the master emotion? How did you answer?

Many people in my seminars say love or confidence or even fear, but no one ever shouts out the right answer: *Purpose is the master emotion.* I think it is because most people see purpose as an outcome or destination. However, purpose is also an emotion. When someone does something meaningful, they will say, "I feel a sense of purpose or I feel purposeful." More importantly, when your thoughts, actions, and emotions are filled with purpose—you will have supreme courage and lose your fear of failure or rejection. When you feel what you are doing is filled with purpose, you will have the extreme confidence to overcome any difficult obstacle or distraction, and all your anxieties will melt away. Purpose is on top of the ladder to all other emotions.

When I discussed emotional toughness in previous seminars, I related it to helping you achieve at a higher level. Obviously, people want to discover how to get into the zone and have a peak performance experience. While audiences liked my message, now they really lean in when I tell stories about how people "fall up" and turn their tragedy into transcendence. Of more significance, they are delighted when I explain that when you have purpose in your actions, you will have supreme emotional and mental toughness. To my surprise and joy, I receive feedback like I never have before in my fifteen years speaking to groups. I can see how this message touches their hearts. Audience members now tell me how they "love" my message and how it impacted their lives in such a meaningful way.

This is the impetus for writing *Fall Up!* At one level, we all want to hear stories about individuals who had severe difficulties yet overcame those hardships and reached their goals. These stories give you the message that your obstacles can be the chisel to free your authentic self. These stories give you hope and inspiration as well as show how you can turn adversity into your super-power for personal growth.

But I want to emphasize that this book is not about tragedy. Let me say that again to be loud and clear. You don't need to have a tragedy to learn from this book, as the essence is about helping you to be filled with that master emotion, every day and in every situation—to make purpose a verb. I want to help you find your recipe for an amazing life. Hopefully, this goal is achieved throughout these pages.

You are an extraordinary person. Greatness is within you. It might have been in hiding, but that is only temporary. If you choose to be the person you always imagined yourself to be—then read on—*Fall Up!* was written for you.

FALL UP!

CHAPTER 1

INTRODUCTION: THE NEW SCIENCE OF SUPER-RESILIENCE

"The eagle never soars in a calm wind."
— Wilbur Wright

AFTER 432 DATES ON MATCH.COM, I FINALLY FOUND THE ONE—TOMMIE. Yes, that is her real name, just in case you were wondering. We fell in love, got married, and, because I was in my late forties at the time, we decided to start a family right away.

So with lots of practice, my lovely wife got pregnant. At the two-month mark, we went to her doctor to get an ultrasound of our baby. The nurse greeted us with a big smile, had Tommie lie on her back, and began to put some type of goo on her belly. The nurse then took this round instrument about the size of her hand and told us to watch the monitor above her head. There we saw the miracle of life—the beating heart of our baby.

We were thrilled, and so we raced home. We began to pick out baby names and colors for the baby room and to buy baby furniture. We began telling all our friends and family about our wonderful news.

Then at the three-month mark, we went back to the doctor. We had the same nurse who put the same goo on Tommie's belly. Except this time, within thirty seconds, her face dropped. She turned to me and said in a deeply saddened voice, "I am so sorry, there is no heartbeat."

Those words felt like someone had just punched me as hard as they could in the stomach. My legs went numb. I looked at Tommie. She was devastated and crying uncontrollably. That made me feel even worse. Then my mind began to race, *Could we handle this pain another time if Tommie were to get pregnant again?* At that moment, I felt hopeless.

But, three months later, Tommie got pregnant again, and today we have an amazing boy, Myles Thomas. We are very blessed. This heart-wrenching experience awoke us to the miracle of life, and now we greatly appreciate every moment with Myles, as we know how special he is to us. He is an amazing gift and the joy of our life.

Why *Fall Up!* Is Always Vital and Pertinent

If you are reading this book, chances are you have had a painful tragedy in your life. Perhaps you got divorced, lost an important job, lost a parent, or a dear friend succumbed to cancer. Or you suffered a miscarriage, as we did. To add fuel to the fire, it seems like social media is reporting a tragedy on a daily basis, from a mass shooting, to a bomb on a plane, to genocide in the Middle East.

Tragedy is unavoidable. Tragedy is part of the human experience. Millions and millions of people are touched by tragedy.

While painful hardships are a part of your journey, they do not have to beat you up and swallow your hope for a wonderful life. Tragedy need not push you down to the darkest feelings of despair. Rather, the tornadoes in your life can help you discover your wings and allow you to soar upward. The eagle was meant to soar in a turbulent wind.

You can fall up!

Adversity Will Propel You Skyward

A tragic moment in David Meador's life became his force for falling up. Twice the national blind golf champion, David speaks to my sport psychology class every semester because he is very jovial and a great speaker. He starts the conversation by telling my class how a blind man plays golf. But then he speaks of the horrific accident. At the age of eighteen, he was driving his car too fast and could not stop as it approached a T in the road. His car crashed into a tree, which in turn smashed his head into the windshield, cracking his skull wide open. When David awoke in his hospital bed, the doctor was standing over him and said these life-changing words: "David, you severed your ocular nerve and you will be blind for the rest of your life."

David then explains to my class that before the accident, he was selfish and uncaring. He had no idea what he wanted to do with his life or who he wanted to become. He was aimless.

But the accident changed him to his core. David tells my students that he became much more focused because he lost his sight. He began to care about others, and his empathy grew exponentially. David proclaims that blindness allowed him to truly see what was important in his life, such as friends and family. He also tells my class that he is the only man in America who can walk through Home Depot and not see a single thing he wants (This always gets a good laugh.).

The Paradigm Shift

David Meador allowed me to see that the old science of loss is incomplete. Most people are familiar with the groundbreaking work of Elisabeth Kübler-Ross. She interviewed people who were dying and discovered they went through distinct stages: anger, denial, depression, bargaining, and, lastly, acceptance. Her work is the gold standard to understand how we can adjust and move through our loss and grief.

While the Kübler-Ross model has captured our attention for decades, it is lacking the final stage of personal growth. People do much more than just move to acceptance. David Meador did not just accept his lot. He did not just bounce back to his original point. He was not just resilient. Rather, he bounced back higher because of his tragedy. He turned his adversity into a super-power for personal growth. David soared skyward and transcended because of the loss of his sight. He turned tragedy into transcendence.

Transcendence is the final stage in tragedy.

It makes sense that transcendence will result from tragedy. Just look at nature itself.

The Nature Factor

Forest fires are the prototypical example of how a tragic event will eventually make the environment more livable for both plants and animals. The tragic fire is a gift to the forest to become stronger for the next generation.

At first glance, it would appear that a fire in the woods would be devastating. But on closer examination, a forest fire can actually benefit the forest and all its inhabitants. A fire cleans the forest floor of debris, which makes the soil more fertile for growth. The fire opens up the existing forest to sunlight, which helps nourish the existing trees. Ultimately, a fire reduces the competition for nutrients, allowing established trees to grow stronger and healthier.

Fire also strengthens the habitat for all the species that live in a forest. Fire clears unwanted brush, which allows new grasses and herbs to regenerate, providing nutrient-rich food for many wildlife species. It also increases the water supply with the removal of unwanted brush. With fewer plants absorbing water, streams are fuller, benefiting all types of plants and animals.

Some species of trees actually *need* forest fires. Certain trees have fire-resistant bark and cones that require heat to open and release seeds for regeneration. Without fire, these trees would eventually succumb to old age, unable to bring new life to the forest.

A devastating fire is actually the lifeblood of the forest and turns the forest into a thriving habitat.

Transcendence Is Built into Our DNA

Transcendence is part of our nature as well. Take the stages of muscle building. Your muscles are more than just resilient. They will continue to grow based on the adversity you place upon them. More specifically, you must expose your muscles to increasing amounts of weight (or resistance) to enhance muscle growth. Once you have exposed your muscles to severe adversity, they will adapt by bringing in extra fluid and protein as a response to the stress placed upon them. More stress must be placed upon the muscles for them to continue their growth stage. This process does not have a ceiling; rather, your body will continue to build and grow as stressors and adversity are placed upon the system.

Interestingly, if you stop placing your muscles into adverse situations, you will lose muscle mass. You have experienced this if you have stopped working out and discovered you can't lift the same amount of weight as before. You need to again go through the rebuilding process. Your DNA makes you an amazing adaptive organism as your muscles can cycle back and forth from adversity to strength.

The New Science of Super-Resilience

Given that transcendence from tragedy happens all around us as well as within us, we must revolutionize our thinking about how people can have an amazing positive transformation from a severe adversity. We must learn the secret to using adversity as a superpower for personal growth. There must be a new science of resilience.

While my academic background and consulting experiences are in resiliency and positive psychology, I had not researched anyone who had used tragedy as a launching pad to greatness— until I started work on this book. I was keenly interested in this new principle, so I interviewed people from all over the world who declared that their tragic moments propelled them forward into the person they were meant to be. As you will see later in the book, I interviewed Kia Scherr, who lost her husband and daughter in a Mumbai terrorist attack, but said that this terrible pain helped her find her true path in life. Because of her tragedy, Kia created a foundation for peace and discovered her life's work. As another example, I sat down with Frankie Caterisano, who told me that she was a severe procrastinator. However, that all changed after a motorcycle accident, which killed her husband and broke both her hips. This painful tragedy propelled her into being an unstoppable person with immense focus and desire. As a result, she went back to college to finish her degree as a physical therapist.

Although *Fall Up!* includes many uplifting true personal stories, more importantly, **this is the first and only book** to share with you the stages for achieving **transcendence**. Amazingly, it was discovered from these interviews that everyone progressed through the same stages to reach transcendence—in the same sequential order. **I call this process "Transcend-Ability," and this is the future for understanding the complete process of resiliency.** The following are the unique stages to reach transcendence, and they create the overall framework for this book:

Stage 1: The Wake-up call

At this stage, adversity awakens you to the realization that you are not on your true path. Some people have described it as if they were sleepwalking through life and hardship awakened them from their slumber.

Stage 2: Flip the switch.

Here, you make the shift to believe the event has a purposeful connection in your life. You begin to realize that you have the power to choose your attitude and see your painful event as an opportunity for personal growth. Once this happens, this tragic event sparks the realization that you must redesign your life for the better.

Stage 3: Release your genius.

When you move into this new direction, you are forced out of your comfort zone. This process helps you to see talents that you never knew existed. You then use these newfound strengths to move to the next step.

Stage 4: Discover your LIFESONG.

At this stage, all the distractions, chaos, and misinformation that had consumed your life turn quiet. Now, you can finally hear your true Lifesong—your life's purpose. Consequently, you live in your flow and find joy and contentment beyond compare.

Stage 5: Make *purpose* a verb.

Discovering your Lifesong is not enough, however. You must take action. When you make *purpose* a verb, you have reached the final stage of transcend-ability. At this final stage, you move from a "me" orientation to a "we" orientation, and your focus turns to having a meaningful impact in the world. Living in your purpose makes you radiate amazing energy, and the world responds in kind. This is the sweet spot in life.

Examples of Transcend-ability

Now that you are aware of the stages of transcendence, you will see these stages everywhere (if you look closely). You will see them in stories of tragedy you read in books or in stories told by the media, and even in people you know.

Take for instance Michael J. Fox. Most people know that the famous actor has Parkinson's disease. It causes severe tremors in his body and limits his ability to speak well. Parkinson's caused Fox to give up his acting career that has made him rich and famous. Most would think that Parkinson's was a terrible tragedy for him.

But true to the stages of transcendence, Michael J. Fox calls his battle with Parkinson's a *gift*. Yes, he sees it as a blessing because it was a wake-up call for him. As he puts it in his autobiography, *Lucky Man*, the gift of Parkinson's allowed him to **flip the switch** and be less selfish and to focus upon his family and the community. He also mentions that Parkinson's forced him to realize his true **purpose** in life: the Michael J. Fox Foundation for Parkinson's research. This foundation is focused on finding a cure for Parkinson's disease as well as promoting the development of therapies to make life better for those living with Parkinson's today. Michael J. Fox made *purpose* a verb by working toward the betterment of mankind rather than just the entertainment of people.

Another prototypical example of the stages of transcendence

that has captured the media's eye is the life story of supermodel Petra Nemcova. While vacationing with her boyfriend at a luxury resort in Thailand, a tsunami pounded their bungalow. The wave took her boyfriend out to sea and he drowned. But by the grace of fortune, the force of water pushed Petra high enough to grab the branches of a palm tree. Battered and bruised from all the debris, she clung on for eight hours, all while she heard the terrified calls of children pleading for help. Petra could not let go of that branch. She knew if she did, she, too, would drown in that death-filled debris. At that moment, she felt completely helpless to save them. But those horrific calls for help were Petra's **wake-up call.**

While recovering from her wounds, both physically and emotionally, Petra began to see that this horrific event had significance in her life. Petra **flipped the switch** and decided that she needed to help children in some way.

Petra returned to Thailand and discovered these children needed new schools. She realized she needed to start a charity to fund this educational goal. This forced her out of her comfort zone, and it allowed her to realize her true genius as an organizer and fundraiser. From this horrific experience, Petra **heard her Lifesong**: She created a charity called All Hands and Hearts. To date, it has opened more than one hundred schools in impoverished areas throughout the world.

At one of the school openings, a young girl came up to Petra and told her, "You are our guardian angel." To Petra, that was one of the most wonderful moments in her life. Because of her tragedy, she achieved transcend-ability as she now lives in purpose, and her life could not be any sweeter.

Both Michael and Petra show us the eternal message of this book: **Tragedy is not meant to diminish you and beat you down; rather, life's hardships are meant to lift you higher. You can fall up to become the person you were meant to be.**

The Journey Is Complete

Knowing the stages of transcendence helps us understand the entire process of being super resilient. This journey to understand resiliency took a long time to complete, but was accomplished when all the pieces fit into an overarching framework. A similar tale involved the discovery of the modern light bulb.

If you are like most people, you probably thought that Thomas Alva Edison invented the light bulb, but that answer is only partially correct. In 1801, the English chemist Humphrey Davy demonstrated that light could be illuminated when platinum strips were heated with electricity inside a glass cylinder. In 1841, Frederick de Moleyns was granted the first patent for what he called "the electric light bulb," and his invention used a charcoal filament. In 1850, Joseph Swan developed a paper filament dipped in a carbon solution. There were at least twenty other inventors from either Europe or America who added to this new invention. However, the main problem with their electric light bulbs was that they functioned only a short time before they went out. None of their light bulbs were feasible for general consumption.

The genius of Thomas Edison was that he had vision—he could see the big picture to this light bulb problem. Edison understood that these inventors only had pieces to this puzzle, but the real picture was far from whole. So Edison improved on their already-existing designs to complete their journey. In 1879, Edison invented the incandescent light bulb using a carbonized bamboo filament that lasted twelve hundred hours, and now our world is lit forevermore.

This Edison tale is very similar to our story of transcendence from tragedy. Many exceptional minds have investigated the science of resiliency and its relation to personal growth. They have tried to understand why some people keep standing when steamrolled by the hard knocks of life while others fall into despair. For example, in his book, *Learned Optimism*, Martin Seligman explains how to become aware of your attributional style. Your attributional style is a personality dimension to how you explain the causes for failure and success. When you become aware of your style, you can change your thinking about failure, and, in turn, become more optimistic and hopeful for the future. Another example is Carol Dweck's popular book *Mindset*, in which she explains how to flip the switch and find the proper mindset in order to see your struggles as a growth opportunity. In his bestselling book, *Go Put Your Strengths to Work*, Marcus Buckingham proposes that to be successful you must become aware of your signature strengths as well as use your signature strengths when confronted with difficult situations. In *When All You've Ever Wanted Isn't Enough*, Harold Kushner tells us that we must be driven by purpose in all life situations if we want to be authentically happy. Craig and Mark Kielburger wrote an amazing book, *Me to We,* which describes the power of connection and its impact upon our happiness. They explain poignantly that we can overcome our hardships when we move from a place of selfishness to a mentality of service. In *Transformed by Trauma*, Tedeschi and Moore illustrate how people can grow in the aftermath of trauma and live great lives.

Unfortunately, many brilliant minds and many wonderful self-help books have only enlightened us to pieces of the whole picture—an unfinished puzzle. They lack the complete vision for harnessing the power of loss, adversity, and hardship. The journey was incomplete—until now.

Fall Up! is the first book that provides a complete picture for blossoming from the bitters. By understanding the stages of transcendence, you will be able to progress through each stage and acquire transcend-ability. With transcend-ability, you will become super-resilient and bounce back higher than you ever thought imaginable. *Fall Up!* shows you how to turn adversity into your super-power for personal growth.

Knowledge gives you this power. The knowledge in this book will give you the power to propel your life to a new dimension. All you need to do is take the first step.

Fall Up! **was written with these five main goals:**

1. Discover the new science of super-resilience. While the Kübler-Ross model had its day in the sunshine, you must move forward and radically change your thinking about resilience. You can do much more than merely accept a loss; you can actually transcend from any difficulty. This is the new science of personal triumph—this is the new science of resilience.

2. Demonstrate the stages of transcendence. These stages are the new science of resilience and create the roadmap to finding your authentic self. Thus, these stages become the chapters for *Fall Up!* These chapters are your essential guide to harness the power of your adversity to become the person you were always meant to be.

3. Illustrate how to turn tragedy into transcendence. An ancient proverb states, "Tell me a fact and I'll learn. Tell me the truth and I'll believe. But tell me a story and it will live in my heart forever." The next chapter is an entertaining parable about a fictitious character, Annie Ainsworth, who moves through the stages to achieve transcend-ability. The parable is then followed by chapters filled with real-life stories of people I interviewed who achieved transcend-ability, as well as stories about people you will recognize from media coverage as well as from history books. The knowledge of how another person has accomplished the Fall Up principle will help you do the same.

4. Demonstrate how to achieve transcend-ability. Transcend-ability is a skill that you can acquire through knowledge and with effective strategies. Each chapter includes useable activities and important tips that will allow you to capitalize on your unique gifts. Because busy people want to make good use of their time, these activities are streamlined for the fast pace of today's world. But don't let the brevity of the activity fool you. Each is packed with a power punch to help you create the life you were meant to live!

5. Find your authentic self. *Fall Up!* is not about tragedy but about finding your true self. If you are not as happy as you want to be—if you are not content in your life—if you are not on your path—then this book is your wake-up call!

Harold Kushner once stated this amazingly powerful truth: "When you have learned how to live, life itself is the reward." The time is now for you to reward yourself by living your Lifesong. This is your truth. It is within your grasp. You can chisel away what is unneeded and discover what is essential. ***Fall Up!* gives you the power to recreate your life into your personal masterpiece.**

CHAPTER 2

BE THE LOVE YOU SEEK
(A PARABLE)

Author's note about the parable:

The parable of Annie Abigail Ainsworth shows us in an entertaining way how adversity helps us to evolve through the stages of transcendence. Enjoy!

"Be the change you wish to see in the world."
— Mahatma Gandhi

FORTUNE SHONE UPON HENRY AINSWORTH'S ACCIDENT. On most nights, he would stagger down the stairs in a drunken stupor to an early bed and an early-morning headache. But on this night, his stars were misaligned and he missed the first step, tumbling down the great flight of stairs until he came to the last step, which gashed open his skull.

Henry Ainsworth lay there bleeding for a few endless hours. No one had heard his terrible fall. Annie, his daughter, who had just come home from an all-night party, found him—as he still miraculously clung to life. The rose-colored wood of the stairs had turned dark with her father's blood, and she knew he had only a few moments to live.

Henry could hear his young daughter weeping with great distress over him. He then summoned all his strength and motioned to Annie to come closer. With quiet desperation, Henry whispered to Annie, "You must go to Bangladesh. You must go to the factory. The secret to your fortune lies in Bangladesh."

Immensely puzzled, Annie asked her dying father, "I don't understand, my father, why Bangladesh?" Henry just repeated in a quiet and desperate tone, "You must go to the city of Tangali in Bangladesh. You will find the answers you seek. I beg of you to go." Those were Henry's final words to his daughter.

One thing was certain, Annie did not want to go to Bangladesh. And Annie always got her way. Annie Abigail Ainsworth was born to one of the wealthiest families on the East Coast. Her family's clothing line, Ainsworth Clothier, was considered one of the best in the world, and with that prestige came more money than can be spent in two lifetimes. And both her parents did spend, and spend, on anything and everything that young Annie wanted—from French dolls to Shetland ponies. Nothing was ever enough.

Then the first tragedy struck young Annie. Veronica Ainsworth, Annie's mother, was always very loving and compassionate toward her young daughter, and she wanted to enrich those same qualities in Annie. As such, Annie's given middle name of Abigail was for the first lady Abigail Adams—wife of the second president, John Adams. Veronica had read of the wonderfully compassionate letters that Abigail had written to her husband. She wanted her daughter to possess that same compassion for the world. Gravely unfortunate, she was never able to nurture those qualities because Veronica died in a terrible car crash when Annie was just seven years old.

Then, as she approached her eleventh year, Annie was bedeviled by a second tragedy. She became afflicted with a mysterious illness that caused her the loss of the use of her right arm. Henry took Annie to every renowned doctor in the country, but none could find a cause or a cure.

With each passing tragedy, Henry showered more and more gifts upon his young daughter. There was a string of new horses and endless amounts of toys. There was frequent European travel: Paris. Rome. London. Annie went to the best schools and had the best tutors. She got everything a child could want.

But like many who never earn what they receive, Annie became immensely spoiled. She would yell at the maids in her home when they misplaced her toys. She would berate the cooks for what she called lousy food. While she loved her father, she would ignore him on many occasions and pretend he did not matter in her life. She was the poster child for spoiled rotten.

Annie was also immensely bitter. Although she was quite beautiful, she could never get past her useless arm. She blamed the world for her problem, usually taking it out on her father and teachers. An exceptionally smart child, she refused to learn the material in school. Always the "problem child" that all the teachers dreaded, Annie got kicked out of more schools than her father could count.

Now at the young age of twenty-five, nothing had changed. She was still spoiled and bitter. She lived a life of pure indulgence. Everything and anything she wanted, she purchased. With endless partying and loveless affairs with men, she had become known for her lack of discretion. She had many friends, but they only cared about her money. She had absolutely no purpose in life, except to perpetuate a hedonistic lifestyle. To date, Annie Abigail had not lived up to her namesake.

Still, Annie wanted to respect her father's dying wish. Although she had travelled all over Europe, she had never been to Bangladesh or even that part of the world. When her father spoke of Tangali—he would always say how happy those families were to have a job making clothes. He emphasized how the company was providing great wealth to that city. So she packed her bags to see it for herself.

When Annie arrived in Bangladesh at the city of Tangali, the company limo picked her up. It had the famous "A" logo plastered on the side of the door. She was shuttled to the main office. Mr. Nisha, a man with a thick, black mustache and gray streaks in his flowing black hair, greeted her on the front steps of the Ainsworth building.

With a saddened tone, Mr. Nisha stated, "I am so sorry for your loss. Your father was a good man." Then as if he had suddenly become a different person, he smiled and welcomed her to his city. He proclaimed he was the foreman of the factory and recommended that they first go see the downtown factory. Then, he suggested, they should get a bite to eat at his favorite restaurant to discuss the future of the company.

To Annie's amazement, the inside of the downtown factory was clean and bubbling with cheer. All the workers seemed happy as they sewed their way to a sweater, shirt, or trousers. As she walked the grounds, she began to see the work that went into each item. Looking at the factory, Annie felt prideful of the Ainsworth name. More importantly, everything and everyone appeared as she had envisioned: a big, glorious company of people, all of whom worked hard to give the Ainsworth products a great name.

Early the next morning at her hotel room, Annie heard a soft knocking. She opened the door to find a young girl about eleven years old standing before her. She had no shoes and dirt covered almost her entire body. Her clothes were not Ainsworth apparel but of rags barely clinging to her body. Incredibly she, too, had the same affliction that bedeviled Annie—her right arm dangled down, useless.

In broken English, the young girl shyly stated, "I am Aaina, and you were deceived by everyone. You did not see the real factory. You have been blinded to what is real here." She then used her bad hand to grab Annie's bad dangling hand and stated, "Come with me, I want to show you—us."

They walked for about a quarter mile until they reached an old dirty factory. As they approached the door, the silence of desperation became louder and louder. As Annie opened the door, her eyes were no longer blinded to the Ainsworth name. For as far as her eyes could see, there were small children chained to their chairs. All were sewing and stitching their hearts out. There was no laughter, no talking, just the sound of little hands being worn out. The "A" logo had become the black mark on their heart. This was a tragedy of epic proportions.

Annie also noticed that many of the girls had the same affliction as she did, with one arm dangling down at the side, useless. In a moment of enlightenment, she realized that she was one of them—only raised in a different world.

Annie then had a more troubling thought: What torment had her family brought upon these people? Just then Annie got sick to her stomach. She could no longer bear witness to the sight of these children slaving away for her company's wealth. She ran out of there as fast as she could go. She ran down the hill until she reached the River Chana, which ran parallel to the town and factory, and gave both its lifeblood.

When she got to the River Chana, Annie gazed upon her reflection in the water's mirror. For the first time, she was disgusted by her image. She was disgusted by her family. She was disgusted by the "A" of her family crest. Everything she had known was a lie.

At that moment, she believed God had not been her companion but had forsaken her. She got down on her knees, looked deep into the river, and began to pray for a message from God.

"Please, give me a sign," she prayed. At this moment in time, Annie felt completely lost in this world.

Just then, Annie heard some rumbling in the bushes behind her. Appearing from out of the bushes was a very, very old man. He was small in stature, not reaching five feet. On the right side of his bald head was a small, dark birthmark in the shape of a dove. He had dark-set eyes, and his skin appeared brown and leatherlike. He walked with a crooked old wooden cane, which helped him to shuffle his little feet, which were bare upon the river's soil, toward her.

With a calming voice, he said, "You must be grateful for the pain—as well as life's pleasure."

Annie looked at him with a puzzled look and thought: *How could he know my pain?*

He spoke again. "You must be grateful for the pain because from it comes your true self. Your life wounds chisel away what is unnecessary and allow your authentic being to appear."

Annie retorted, "Who are you, old man?"

He replied in a calming voice, "My name is Ohna, and I live here at the river. Some have said I am the guardian of the river. This river is the love you seek. I know you have hardship in your heart at this moment, but this pain is the light that will split your heart wide open. What you have experienced today is the light that will shine on you for the rest of your life."

"No one has spoken like that to me before," Annie said. "There is pain in my heart right now, the same pain I felt when I began losing the use of my right arm. I just don't see how this pain can be helpful and how the loss of my arm helped me in any way. I am not sure of anything right now."

Annie then said, "But I can see you are a very wise old man; and I am completely lost at what I need to do—so I will listen."

"Come here tomorrow to this spot," Ohna said. "We will

start. All it takes is the first step, and you will find out who you are and who you really can be. Enough said today."

Ohna then tapped his cane three times on the ground and spoke these words, "Be the love you seek." He disappeared into the deep brush from where he had magically appeared just moments earlier.

That afternoon, Annie went to pay Mr. Nisha a visit at the Ainsworth building.

"Why did you lie to me?" Annie asked.

"About what did I lie?" Mr. Nisha answered.

"The factory you showed me is a lie. I saw the real one with all the children chained to their chairs, slaving away at the clothes. It made me sick to my stomach. It is horrific."

"I showed you what you wanted to see—like all the rest from America—all they ever want is the happy cheerful company of Ainsworth clothing, and then they are on their way back home," Mr. Nisha said. "I thought you were like all the rest. I did not think you wanted the truth." He then paused and added, "I did not think you could handle the truth."

"I want the truth. What else don't I know?" Annie asked.

"There are three more factories like the one you saw, all scattered around Bangladesh," Mr. Nisha said in a harsh tone.

"Three more—oh my God—that is unbearable," Annie said tenderly.

"The clothing business is highly competitive. How do you think we beat the competition every year—by our designs? No, of course not. It all comes with our cheap labor. Look, we give those children a small wage once a month and feed them. Is that so terrible?"

"Yes," Annie replied, and, after a long pause, she asked the dreaded question for which she needed to know the answer: "Was my father aware of this tragedy?"

"I have been the foreman for five years, and your father never visited our town, so I am not sure." Mr. Nisha paused, and then asked, "But how could he not know?"

And with those words, Annie left the building as her heart cried out once again.

The next morning Annie went back to the River Chana. She looked deep into the river, but this time, at this moment, her image was murky. She kneeled down at its edge and asked, "Why am I here—must I be tormented by these images?"

She felt a presence standing behind her. It was Ohna leaning on his crooked cane.

"Listen to the river closely. The rumbling of the rushing water. It has its own harmony," the old one said. "Like the River Chana that rushes before you, life has its own flow—its own harmony. The events in your life play out like notes of your Lifesong. Every moment of your life has been sung to you for a reason. This is the great universal symphony."

Ohna then finished: "You saw what you needed to see because you are now ready to hear this song. Each event is its own teacher, and now you are ready for the lesson. This is your wake-up call and now you must listen."

Annie stood up embarrassed, and she interrupted: "I was always a terrible student because I never really cared about life. I just went through the motions. I never really cared for anything because it was all given to me at my every whim. So far, I have been sleepwalking through my life."

Ohna stepped close to Annie, and in his most heart-filled voice, said, "Care is the essence of the human spirit. Without caring or compassion in your heart, you go through life without a melody. All the notes of your life will never connect. Your Lifesong will never be heard."

Ohna added firmly, "Annie, you hold the title to your thoughts.

You did not care because you chose not to care. You must take responsibility for your choices. Now you must make the shift and change the song that continually plays in your head. You must let go of the pain and forgive who you believe has caused you wrong. You have the power to flip the switch, and with that power comes your ability to see life in all its grandeur."

He continued. "What you have seen here in Bangladesh has significance. You must see all these events that have played before you as a reason to change your Lifesong. You must awaken your heart to the truth. When you do that, your life will harmonize with everything and everyone. Like the flowing River Chana at your feet, you will finally and eternally feel the rushing of life in your veins."

Ohna then added, "Come back here under the dawn's first light and we will move in the direction you need." He tapped his cane three times and hushed these words: "Be the love you seek." Then he vanished into the forest next to the river.

Later that day, Annie decided to see the township of Tangali with her own eyes. Aluminum-bound, one-room houses dotted the sides of the dirt roads. Trash was strewn everywhere she looked—on the streets, next to the houses, and even on their rooftops. Goats, dogs, and chickens roamed the area freely, as if they ran the town. The smell of extreme poverty was everywhere.

Interestingly, no one seemed to notice Annie. Perhaps they were afraid of strangers, or ashamed of what she saw, but no one said a word and just let her pass unnoticed.

Just then, Aaina appeared in front of her and grabbed her hand. "Come" was all she said. They walked together up the hill until they reached a very small hutlike structure. "My house—come," Aaina said in her broken English.

There at the table sat her mother, father, and two sisters. They were about to eat dinner, which consisted of flattened bread and some type of bean-looking substance. Aaina said, "Sit and eat."

Sitting there and eating dinner with this family, Annie realized the true sting of poverty. Five beings lived in this one-room structure, with no windows or running water. They all slept on the dirt floor, around this table at which they presently sat.

Annie had been blinded to all this back on Long Island Sound. This world was the polar opposite of how she grew up. Now she knew how the other half lived. She was appalled and broken-hearted at the same time.

Annie thanked Aaina for the meal and hospitality, and went back to her hotel to digest everything she saw and felt.

The next morning, Annie heard a pounding at her door. Mr. Nisha stood before her and asked if he could come in to discuss a business proposal. He said he had met with the board of directors, and they were willing to buy her out of her share of the company for $10.5 million. In a degrading tone, he added, "You don't know how to run a company; you have no idea how this company needs to be run. You have lived a cushy American life. This money will allow you to live carefree for the rest of your life. Take this offer and never look back. We will take care of these children and this town. The conditions will change, I promise you."

Annie seemed pensive and simply said, "That is a very generous offer from you and the board. Let me think this over," and with those words Mr. Nisha left.

The next morning at dawn, Annie headed down to the River Chana for some inspiration and words of wisdom from Ohna. She looked all over for him, but Ohna was not by the river's edge. She called out, but heard nothing.

Then, as she was about to leave, Annie heard Ohna's voice from across the river. He was leaning on his crooked cane and said to her, "Swim across to this side."

Annie yelled to him, "Can't you see that I have only one good arm and the current is strong. I will never make it across." But more importantly, Annie knew she was scared to swim across to the other side.

Ohna simply said, "You must take a leap of faith and believe."

At this point, Annie trusted Ohna and knew he was wise, so she jumped in. The current was strong and with only one good arm, she kept getting pulled under the water. She bobbed up for a few seconds and then was pulled under again. Over and over it happened. Then by chance she grabbed onto a vine and pulled herself back to shore. The river had beaten her. She was exhausted.

She looked and Ohna was still on the other side waiting for her. She was too tired to speak and walked sheepishly back to the hotel, soaked with dejection.

The next morning, Annie heard a pounding at the door. Again it was Mr. Nisha. But this time, he was more abrasive with his words. "You will take this offer because you have no choice. The board will drive you out of this company."

He added, "We all believe you would bring this company to ruins. All our lives would be ruined if you don't take this offer." With a look she had never seen, he stated, "You will be sorry if you don't," and then he left.

This time, Annie felt scared for her safety and for the future. She did not know what Mr. Nisha was capable of or whether she could even run the company. She had been sheltered all her life.

How could I run such a big company? Perhaps Mr. Nisha and the board are correct, Annie thought. She did not know what to do, but she felt the pull from the river, so that is where she went.

She kneeled by the river and prayed, "God, what should I do? I need guidance."

Just then Ohna appeared on the other side of the river leaning on his crooked cane, and told her, "You must swim across to this side."

"I tried yesterday and failed!" Annie shouted back dejectedly.

"Take a leap of faith and swim across. You must believe," Ohna told her again.

Annie dove into the river and began to paddle as hard as she could with her one good arm. Again she went under the water because the current was so powerful. But she kept on kicking and paddling. She thought it was impossible, but she did not give up. She just kept going and going as hard as she could. Just then she felt a vine touch her shoulder and so she began to pull—she pulled with all her might, and, to her amazement, she had reached the other side, exhausted yet exuberant.

Ohna was standing above her leaning on that crooked cane and told her, "You see, you have the gift. There are talents hidden deep inside of you that you had no idea existed. They have lain dormant, but now they are awakened. It is only with hardship that you can truly see yourself. Today, I hope you see you are capable of the impossible. You can make the impossible possible."

"I can't believe I really made it," Annie said joyfully.

"I had no doubt in you—the River Chana had no doubt in you. Now you must have no doubt in what you can do!" the old wise one said in a heartfelt tone.

"Everyone treated me like I could not do anything because I had only one arm. I always believed them. My father and teachers made me think I would fail if I tried anything difficult, so I was just given everything, and in turn, I received nothing of value," Annie said. "But now I can see clearly. I believe I am capable."

Annie looked into the river to gaze upon her reflection. This time she saw a glow in the water's mirror. She could not describe it, but it seemed as if her reflection had changed—as if true joy resonated from her image.

Ohna put his hand on Annie's shoulder and said, "You were able to cross the river for a reason. Your inner strength is beyond measure. That now should be apparent. You have come far today.

"Enough said today."

He then tapped his cane three times and said, "Be the love you seek." Ohna then pointed to a bridge up the road about a quarter mile and told her that the next lesson would begin at sunrise at the bush of rainbows. He disappeared into the forest next to the river's edge.

That evening Annie asked everyone at the hotel if they knew of the bush of rainbows. No one had heard of it or knew of its existence. Then at dinner, a young busboy, who walked with a slight limp, came up to her and said, "Please don't tell anyone that I am telling you this. I go to the bush of rainbows when I feel sadness in my heart. The bush of rainbows appears where the river bends. Look to your right and you will see an opening in the forest, and above the opening the flowers appear red, blue, yellow, green, purple—every color of the rainbow."

Then he left without being thanked for his gift of knowledge.

At sunrise the next morning, Annie found the bush of rainbows where the river bends. There, leaning on his crooked cane, was Ohna.

He said to follow him into the forest. The path began to climb upward, but Ohna did not slow down. They climbed up on this path for another hour, not saying a word to each other. Then they came to a clearing in the brush.

Ohna stopped and said, "We have arrived at our vantage point. From here you can see the whole town. You can see the factory and the river. From here, you can see the real beauty of this place. I have seen the sun rise and set many times over Tangali from this spot." He then stopped for a moment, took a deep breath, and soaked in the view.

"I grew up here," Ohna continued. "So did my parents and their parents before them. Our seed has been sown on this ancient fertile plain. I feared the love here had been spoiled—until

I saw you at the river. I knew then that life's giving radiance had come."

Ohna added, "Each must take the path destined for us. I have mine, you have yours, and your father had his and his father, too."

Annie was completely taken aback from what Ohna had just told her. She said, "You met my father, and my grandfather, too?"

"Thirty years ago, your father had come to the river, and I spoke to him," Ohna said. "Thirty years before that, his father had come to the river, and I spoke to him. My words had no meaning to them. Their hearts could not hear me for they beat at a different vibration. I could not move them toward love. They chose their own path, as you must choose."

"But how do I know which is the right path for me? How can I know for sure?" Annie said.

Ohna raised his cane and pointed to the heavens and shouted, "Your truth is undeniable—it oozes from your being!" He finished with, "I must go now. You can find your own way back."

Annie spoke cautiously: "There are so many paths down. I am not sure which one to pick. I can't remember how we got here. I surely will get lost."

Ohna looked deep into her eyes and said, "You will know the right path because when you are on it, an overwhelming sense of serenity will take hold of you. You will feel the universe in complete alignment with your being. You will feel connected to everyone and everything. Enough said." He then tapped his cane three times and spoke the words, "Be the love you seek," and disappeared into the forest.

As Annie walked down the mountain, she began to know the feeling of peace of which Ohna had spoken. It was the right path home.

Annie now knew in her heart what she must do. She marched over to the Ainsworth building and right up to Mr. Nisha's office.

When he opened the door, Annie stated emphatically, "I am going to run this company. My name is on our clothes, not yours or the board's. I will do what is right—and my first step is to fire you. Please get your stuff and leave my building," and with those words she left and went back to the hotel to pack for home.

As she was packing for New York to start her new life, Annie again felt a very strong pull to go to the River Chana. She stopped what she was doing and headed there.

Ohna was waiting at the river's edge, leaning on his crooked cane. He started with, "My heart breaks today as this is our last lesson together—I will not see you again for a long time. But this lesson is the key to your happiness. Come here next to me, Annie." Then Ohna placed his hand into the bad hand of Annie's.

He completed his truth with, "Your hardship shone a bright light upon your life. You now know you have the power to choose your thoughts. Your true gifts have been awakened in you. And you can now hear the true song of your life. But all is for naught, unless" . . . he paused for a moment . . . "unless you have love in your heart."

"This arm that I hold in my hand is your essence," Ohna continued. "This is why you are here—this wonderful arm brought you to me. You must see that your arm is what makes you special. Your arm did not beat you down, but rather it lifted you up. Your life wounds have led to your transcendence—to a higher state of being—to a higher state of purpose."

Annie just nodded as a tear welled up in her right eye.

Ohna finished the lesson with: "Love is the way. When you love yourself and everything about you, then and only then can you truly love others around you. And it is the love for others that is the true treasure in our lives. This kind of love will bust you open into a new galaxy of emotion. Our love and compassion for others is what lifts us up to an amazing vantage point where only beauty and serenity reign in our heart. Enough said today."

29

He then tapped his cane three times and told her, "Today and forever—be the love you seek," and with that, Ohna disappeared into the forest one last time.

Back in New York, it all seemed like a wonderful dream. Four years had passed since Annie had spoken to Ohna on the river's edge, but his words still resonated loudly within her thoughts and in all her actions.

The company had been transformed under her loving eye. Annie had gotten rid of the old worn-out factories in Bangladesh and replaced them with modern facilities and equipment. She had created educational programs for the adult workers to harness their talents on the machinery.

No children were allowed to work, but rather Annie had begun to build schools for all the children in that country. More importantly, all Ainsworth schools were free to all children who wanted to attend and learn. It seemed as if a new school were being built each month in Bangladesh to support all the needs there.

The Ainsworth brand had been transformed from being known for prestige and wealth into a brand of world change. Consumers began to see the "A" as a mark for giving and making the world a better place. People from all over the world now wanted to work at Ainsworth Clothier, and the company had become a movement instead of just a successful business.

Annie had become the talk of the town. People wanted to meet her and speak to her about her thoughts and her plans. She had more friends than she could count; and, this time, none cared about her money, only about Annie—the person.

But the greatest pride, and most dear to her heart, was the creation of the Veronica Bell Foundation. The "soul" purpose of this foundation was to eradicate the affliction that had affected Annie since childhood. The goal of this foundation was to develop a simple vaccination that could be administered around the world to all children. The vaccination was in its early stages of development, but progress was pushing forward fast.

Annie, too, had made an amazing transformation. She now lived in purpose every day and had transcended into a beautiful being. She felt a sense of peace and tranquility in her life now, a feeling she really never had before. The bitterness in her heart had evaporated; joy and contentment flowed in its place. She had come to realize that her father's words were true. The secret to her life rested in Bangladesh. Ohna's words were founded in truth as well: "True fortune lies in giving and caring about others—love is the way."

Yet on this day in her New York office, Annie felt a powerful yearning. She had a strong feeling that something was missing, but she was unclear of its origin. She looked at her image in the mirror—and staring back at her was the River Chana. She could again feel the pull of the river in her heart.

Annie knew she needed to go back to Bangladesh, to Tangali, to the River Chana to find Ohna—and thank him. She had never really thanked him for all he had done for her. So she packed her bags.

When Annie arrived at Tangali, she went down to the river and shouted his name, but no one came. For a week, every morning and afternoon, she went to the river and into the town looking for him, but Ohna was nowhere to be seen or found. She asked everyone if they had seen the old man with the crooked cane. No one had ever seen him or knew of him.

Then one morning there was a knock at her hotel door. It was Aaina. She had grown into a beautiful young girl. She told Annie, "I know of the old man with the crooked cane, and I can show you where he is."

Annie was impressed. Aaina spoke English well now and Annie told her so. Aaina replied that she was now going to the new Ainsworth School, and her English was improving rapidly. There was a tug at Annie's heart.

Aaina then grabbed her hand and led her to the river. From there they climbed up the path. For more than an hour they climbed. They came to a clearing in the brush, and to a vantage point looking over the town. Annie just then remembered that this was the same clearing that Ohna had shown her years before.

All of a sudden Annie felt the presence of Ohna standing behind her. She turned to greet him. To her astonishment, Ohna was standing there . . . but he was in the form of a statue. It was Ohna leaning on his crooked cane; now carved in stone.

"Ohna!" Annie cried out.

"Yes, this is Ohna," Aaina said. "He is the guardian angel of our town. He has been here for longer than anyone can remember. From this vantage point, he watches over us."

Just then Annie noticed some numbers and words that were carved underneath the statue. Annie could not believe her eyes. It read "Ohna: born 1620, died 1715." Ohna had stood there for centuries watching over the River Chana and those souls that touched its shores.

Annie then noticed some other words that she could not read underneath his statue, as they were in Aaina's native language. Annie asked her to read them to her.

"Ohna tells us . . . **'Be the love you seek.'**"

Author's note about the parable:

This parable parallels the stages of transcendence and illustrates the process of developing transcend-ability. Annie has her wake-up call when she visits Tangali and sees that her family business uses child labor to build its profits. There she meets Ohna, who helps her understand that she always has the power to choose her attitude and see her painful event as an opportunity for personal growth. Because Annie flips the switch, she gets out of her comfort zone to uncover hidden strengths and talents that laid dormant in her, such as great fortitude and confidence. These experiences in Tangali allow Annie to hear her Lifesong: She was transformed from a spoiled and bitter person to someone who is committed to make a difference in the world around her. Annie now lives in purpose, and her life exemplifies the true principles of Fall Up.

However, the true essence of the parable happens at the ending. We discover that Ohna was always a statue. Ohna represents eternal wisdom. Annie always had this eternal wisdom within her. Annie always had transcend-ability within her. **You Are The Same As Annie.** You have eternal wisdom within you. You have the ability to discover your authentic self and hear your Lifesong. But most importantly, you always have the power to take action. As Ohna told us in the parable, **"Be the love you seek."** Ohna wants you to **"be"** and take action toward turning your life into a masterpiece.

The following pages in this book are here to enlighten you as well as guide you through this process.

CHAPTER 3

THE WAKE-UP CALL

"What is necessary to change a person
is to change his awareness of himself."

— Abraham Maslow

H IDDEN IN OUR SOCIAL CONSCIOUSNESS, **THE WAKE-UP CALL** LAYS THE FOUNDATION for many of our books as well as it creates many of the themes for our favorite movies. The perennial movie favorite, *The Wizard of Oz*, uses the storyline that the struggles in Dorothy's journey awakens her to her authentic self and pushes her to become the person she was always meant to be.

At first glance, *The Wizard of Oz* appears to be amazingly entertaining and creative. With so many memorable characters, such as the Munchkins, the Scarecrow, and Glinda the Good Witch, it is hard to pick a favorite. *The Wizard of Oz* is also an amazing musical with such timeless tunes as "Over the Rainbow," sung by Dorothy dreaming of a better future. And who could not love the Cowardly Lion barking out, "If I were king of the forest." Every song and dance captures your imagination and complements each scene as if both needed each other. It is one of those rare movies that you never want to end.

But *The Wizard of Oz* is more than just a song and dance. This unique movie captures our hearts because it speaks eternal truths of the human condition. At a much deeper and engaging level, this movie represents a journey of self-discovery. Dorothy's journey on the yellow brick road is actually her journey of self-awareness. This is where the Scarecrow, Tin Man, and the Cowardly Lion come into the symbolic mix. The Scarecrow represents intelligence, the Tin Man personifies compassion, and the Cowardly Lion signifies courage. Together, these characters symbolize essential qualities that Dorothy needs on her journey to grow up—to become the person she is meant to be.

By the movie's end, the Great and Powerful Oz pulls back the curtain and enlightens the audience to an essential truth of the human condition. The Wizard gives the Scarecrow a paper diploma for his smarts; the Tin Man gets a ticking watch as his heart, representing compassion; and the Cowardly Lion receives a badge of courage. However, these were only symbolic gestures—the Wizard just made them become aware of the characteristics each had always had.

In essence, this same truth applied to Dorothy. She always had these qualities (smarts, courage, and compassion), but it was her struggles with the Wicked Witch that released her true strengths and freed her authentic self. **It was Dorothy's hardships that propelled her to Fall Up.**

You are just like Dorothy! You will face many tornadoes and wicked witches on your journey. At times, these life setbacks will seem quite unfair and appear insurmountable and unconquerable. And like Dorothy, these hardships will be your **wake-up call** to "go home" and find your true path—your "yellow brick road." **The first stage of achieving transcend-ability is the wake-up call,** and this process extends far beyond the silver screen.

Frankie Caterisano was awakened to her true path one fate-filled night on the back of a motorcycle. During her college years, she loved to ride on the back of the motorcycle, especially when her husband, Mark, took the corners or sharp turns. It was quite thrilling to feel the momentum of the bike glide along the pavement. Until that one moment that irrevocably changed both their young lives.

On the last turn for home, a drunk driver veered into their lane, hitting their bike straight on with immense speed. Her husband took the brunt of the smash and died instantly. Fortunately, Frankie took only a glancing blow and was thrown thirty yards onto the sidewalk.

When Frankie awoke in the hospital, the doctor told her that her pelvis was crushed and that it was highly unlikely she would ever walk again. For three months, she lay in her hospital bed, heartbroken and reliving that terrible accident, over and over again in her mind.

But that life-changing moment became her **wake-up call**. As Frankie told me, "Mark was unstoppable. Nothing would deter him from his goals in life. I, on the other hand, was the prototypical procrastinator. I always looked for excuses not to finish something or achieve my dreams. Amazingly, it was if Mark's soul went into mine, and I realized that I now needed to be unstoppable like him."

Frankie's turn with tragedy created a turn toward transcendence in her life. She now felt unstoppable. While always smart, she was not adamant about college and using her talents. Though she had to drop out of college for six months because of the accident, nothing would deter her from her Lifesong. Frankie finished her degree as a physical therapist so she could help others with similar physical difficulties. By the way, Frankie walks with only a slight limp when she goes to visit her clients, which typically starts an interesting dialogue about how to stay focused on your goals.

Frankie's story is not unique. History is lined with stories of people whose emotional suffering chimed as a wake-up call. Their darkness forced them to become unstoppable in reaching their dreams—to discover their Lifesong. One amazing example in history was the life of Samuel Morse.

The Historic Wake-up Call

While most know his name from the famous communication code he developed, what is lesser known is that Samuel Morse had an incredible talent as a painter. Originally, he had planned to make a living as a portrait artist, and he was quite good at it. He painted Lafayette as well as President James Monroe. But those plans changed when his wife and love of his life, Lucretia, passed away. Samuel Morse was not, however, at her side. Rather, he was three hundred miles away painting portraits. Unfortunately, and tragically, he did not get the news in time to say good-bye to his dying wife. Morse was completely heartbroken.

The pain of that loss and his inability to be at her side in her last moments haunted him for the rest of his life. But his tragedy became his **wake-up call** to discover a faster way to communicate than by carrying the news on horseback. Morse made it his mission to find a better way so that others would not suffer the same fate he had.

Besides being an artist, Morse also had a talent in science. While studying at Yale, he was exposed to the new field of electricity and its fundamentals. Morse began to understand the physical properties of electromagnetic currents. But that was only the first step. By chance, on a voyage back from Paris, he met another voyager who was experimenting with electromagnets as a form of communication. Morse now had an epiphany and realized he could use this new science to design a technology to create instantaneous communication.

As history has been written, Samuel Morse created his famous communication code with different electrical impulses representing symbols. In certain combinations, those dots and dashes represent different letters, leading to a signal that could be sent across a wire. The person on the other end of the wire would hear the message being transmitted via taps and pauses, write it down, and then decode it into words. Morse's new technological invention allowed a message to be sent at the speed of light instead of by the speed of the horse. Fantastically, his tragedy still inspires us today as his communication framework acts as the foundation for our computers.

The Emotional Bottom Sparks the Wake-up Call

The painful tragedy of Samuel Morse inspired him to sail into our history books. Many people who were interviewed for this book felt a similar moment of inspiration from their tragedy. Remarkably, many stated that it was if they were sleepwalking through life and their emotional pain acted like a slap in the face. Their hardship awakened them from their slumber of living an unhappy and unfulfilled life. Such is the story of Sam Russell.

As a young man, Sam Russell moved from Texas to Hollywood to be a fashion stylist for the rich and famous. This was always his dream. He loved clothes and being around celebrities and pretty people. But Sam was always finding himself in destructive, abusive relationships. On one unfortunate night while driving, his significant other hit him in the face out of anger. Sam lost control of his car and swerved into oncoming traffic on a very busy highway. By sheer luck, no one died. But that near-death experience became his **wake-up call** as it opened his eyes as well as his mind. A repressed memory had awakened from the deepest recesses of his mind. Sam had been sexually abused by his uncle.

While this repressed memory revealed to him why he was in one bad relationship after another, it also placed a direct spotlight upon his life. Sam began to look at his life at a deeper level. He realized that being in Hollywood was not his true life trajectory or end point.

While he was financially successful as a clothes stylist for the Hollywood stars, Sam now felt a dark hole in his life. The tragedy forced him to come to the realization that hanging with the movers and shakers of the entertainment world no longer fulfilled his essence. He needed to shift to a more meaningful direction. He had no choice. A change cried out to be heard.

Sam Russell's genius resided in his ability to fit people perfectly for clothes. As he put it, "I could see their soul and outfit them to a tee. I now knew I needed to harness this strength for the common good. I am meant for a greater purpose in the lives of others."

The new Lifesong for Sam Russell was to create a charity called the Giving Closet. Because of his wonderful connections, the best clothes and jewelry worn by actors in Hollywood movies are donated to this charity. Of more significance, the Giving Closet donates a $10,000 wardrobe to a woman in dire straits so that she can get a job and get back on her feet. Sam uses his genius to make this deserving person look professional and feel wonderful, both on the outside and from within.

Sam Russell feels that this is his destiny and said that there is no greater pleasure than to see a woman's face light up when she has the right wardrobe. Sam can see the transformation in each of these women and this gives him immense joy and positive energy. Sam's tragedy was the painful slap that forced him to find his sweet spot in life.

Your Physiology Acts as a Wake-up Call

While an awakening can come when you hit emotional rock bottom, as it did for Sam Russell, your wake-up call can also result from being out of sync with your authentic self. This is a common occurrence as well as a universal tragedy. When you are not following your true path, you intuitively know it. Your subconscious knows it, and as a result, this discomfort can erupt in many ways. It might come in the physical form as intense headaches or a session of acne. This circumstance of being out of balance with your Lifesong can also develop into insomnia, sadness, or severe bouts of anxiety.

Your physiology will scream out to you when you are not on your true path. You just need to listen.

My **wake-up call** came with a severe bout of anxiety that I would regularly experience at 3:30 in the morning. Like an alarm clock, I would awaken in the middle of the night with a feeling of dread and panic. It would feel like I was in a dark hole of depression. The pit in my stomach went to my throat. My heart would palpitate and my hands would tremble. But, like clockwork, I would close my eyes, take a couple of deep breaths, and after a few minutes, that palpable feeling of despair would leave me.

I did not understand why I had this dark emotion. I had a great job as a professor and greatly enjoyed teaching college students. I played golf almost every day and was working on becoming a great amateur player. This time in my life should have felt like a fine wine, smooth and easy.

Then I got my wake-up call one Tuesday afternoon—when I saw Dr. Phil on *The Oprah Winfrey Show*. He was speaking to a woman who was struggling in her marriage. She was describing the same exact feelings I had, and they were occurring at roughly the same time in the early morning hours. Dr. Phil told her that her body was screaming out to her for a change. She was in a bad relationship with her husband and her physiological response was her wake-up call for a change.

This was my awakening. I now realized that I was in a bad relationship with my work. But until that moment I did not realize it.

Yes, being a college professor is a good life, but there is a superficiality to it. Most professors will tell you that students primarily want to know three main points:

1. Is this going to be on the test?
2. How can I get an "A" in the class?
3. Do I really have to buy the book?

I needed a deeper connection than that. I needed to realign my career. I needed to adjust my path and discover my true Lifesong.

I have a very creative soul and was not using this strength in my career. While I was teaching college students the basics, I needed to expand my message to a larger, more mature audience. So I began to write books on emotional development and speak throughout the country to associations, organizations, and businesses about purpose and happiness.

Once this happened, that feeling at 3:30 went away. It vanished because my true Lifesong was, and is, to share with the world my wisdom about personal development and help audiences find their own Lifesong.

I knew I was in my sweet spot when I received a letter one day from a Nicaraguan priest. It was written in Spanish, so I had to decode it on Google. But those words transcended any language. The opening was as sweet as anything I had ever read, as it said: "God bless you, Dr. Steinberg, for writing *Flying Lessons.*"

This was my second book about showing parents and teachers how to build mental and emotional toughness in children for school, sport, and life. He asked in the letter if he could use my book, which had a Spanish version, in his church schools.

The letter gave me such a feeling of authentic joy. No round of golf ever gave me such immense happiness. I framed that letter and posted it in my office, and I still look at it every day. I had re-aligned my life to be filled with the sweet feeling of purpose.

Like Frankie Caterisano, Samuel Morse, Sam Russell, and my-self, most people are unaware of the depths to which their darkness has grown. Unless your physiology calls to you or you suffer a se-vere hardship or painful tragedy, most people will continue to sleepwalk through their lives. Your true Lifesong will lie slumber-ing out of reach of your awareness without a wake-up call.

But you can awaken to your life and discover your "yellow brick road"! This essential skill is within your grasp. Henry David Thoreau once stated, "In the long run, men (people) hit only where they aim." I would add: "We need to become aware of where to aim." The following activities will help give you a wake-up call so that you aim your life in the right direction:

1. Develop a higher level of emotional intelligence.

This is one of the key steps to self-awareness, but this process is not new. The ability to master your emotions was prized as far back as ancient Greece. Plato used the term *sophrosyne* to de-scribe the ability to value fortune and disaster in the same light. The Greek philosophers cherished a tempered balance, and they believed qualities such as self-mastery and self-control would transcend time as essentials for a prosperous life.

In today's literature, Daniel Goleman has popularized this same notion in his seminal book, *Emotional Intelligence* (EQ).

Goleman has proposed that two essential qualities of EQ are emotional awareness and emotional control. EQ is an essential ingredient to discovering your true path in life.

While there are many methods to enhancing your EQ, one of the first steps is to get in tune with your emotions on a daily basis. To accomplish this, get an EQ journal and begin to record how you feel about interactions, tasks, etc. I know it sounds simple, but this process is very powerful for developing a greater sense of your emotions and how they impact your decisions and behaviors. When this happens, you are on your way to enhancing your EQ.

2. Always ask why.

Ted Williams, known as the greatest natural baseball hitter of all time, always focused his attention on swinging the lumber. Ted Williams wanted to know as much as he could about hitting. Figuratively, he wanted to get a PhD in the science of hitting. In his autobiography, *My Turn at Bat*, Williams wrote, "I want to know why. I think *why* is a wonderful word."

Fall in love with the word *why*. Each day ask yourself five "whys" about your life.

Why did I act this way when my spouse made that statement? Why did I respond that way to my child? Why did I cry when I read that passage in the book?

These questions and their respective answers will lead you to a greater level of self-awareness.

3. Your future self

Listening to your future self is a very powerful awareness tool. The first step is to imagine that you can go back in time and speak to your high school self. What advice would you give your high school self? What answers would you give your high school self to the following questions:

1. What should I major in, in college?
2. What profession is best for me?
3. What type of person should I marry?
4. What strengths do I have that I don't know about?

Now, take it one step further and imagine you meet yourself twenty years into the future. What pearls of wisdom would this future self give you today? What answers would your future self give you to the following questions:

1. Am I on my true path?
2. How can I be happier?
3. What should I change in my life?
4. Am I using my true strengths?

All the wisdom you need is within you. You just need a prompt to access it!

4. Harmonizing activities
Which activities place you into flow?

That is, which activities place you into flow so that when you are doing them, you lose track of time, and are emotionally engaged. List at least three activities.

_____

_____

_____

Next, ask yourself "why" these activities place you into flow. The activities that place you into flow shine a light onto activities that give you meaning and purpose. Once discovered, you need to add these activities into your life on a regular basis. This includes in your work and in all aspects of your life.

5. Energizing activities

Teddy Roosevelt, one of our greatest presidents, thrived on risk. In one of his now-famous speeches, he said, "Far better it is to dare mighty things to win glorious triumphs even though checkered by failure than to take rank with those poor spirits who neither enjoy much nor suffer much because they live in the gray twilight that knows not victory nor defeat." From history we know that Teddy thrived on risk, from riding up San Juan Hill with the Rough Riders to busting trusts and monopolies. He found his true path when he filled his life with action-packed activities.

Do you thrive on risks? Do you enjoy driving fast in the rain? Have you bungee jumped?

What activities get you pumped up? What activities inspire you and give you great positive energy? List three:

_____

_____

_____

Next, ask yourself "why" these activities give you great energy. Activities that give you great positive energy act as clues to your authentic self. Once discovered, you need to add these activities into your life on a regular basis, both at work and in aspects of your life outside work. When accomplished, you will be moving in the right direction to creating your life filled with song.

6. Negative energizing activities

If you are like I am, doing high-risk activities gives you heartburn. I try to avoid high-risk stuff like the plague. As such, you must discover which activities drain you. Same as with the activities that pump you up. Also ask yourself "why" these activities drain you. This helps bring awareness to your authentic self.

Once discovered, remove these activities from your life.

7. Why do you choke?

Besides becoming aware of activities that drain you, you need to know why you choke (perform at your worst at inopportune times). Write down three events in which you performed very poorly:

_____

_____

_____

Now, address why you choked during these events. Was it because you worried about what others thought of you? Was it because you tried to be perfect?

Knowing why you performed at your worst helps you to avoid the wrong path in life.

8. Emotional hot buttons

Carl Jung once said, "Everything that irritates us can lead us to an understanding about ourselves." Next time you have a few conversations with a significant other or loved one, write down the statements that upset you. These statements are your red flags as they are pushing your emotional hot buttons. Look closely at these red flags and you will gain a much-greater glimpse of what is blocking you from reaching your true potential and finding your sweet spot in life.

9. Do you self-handicap?

French chess champion Alexandre Deschappelles had great insecurities about his abilities. To remedy this, he would only play an opponent if that person would remove one of Deschappelles's pawns and then make the first move. Thus, he would not look like a fool if he lost. His ploy supported his fragile ego. Psychologists have labeled this phenomenon as self-handicapping.

Do you self-handicap? Do you create obstacles in your life so you don't achieve your goals? Do you engage in activities so that you never hear your Lifesong?

Becoming aware of your self-handicapping strategies is an essential step to removing them from your life. And with their removal, you are more likely to discover your authentic self.

10. Outside the box

There is a psychological principle that states, "It is hard to know what the picture looks like when you are inside the frame." In many cases, it is quite difficult to really know what your self-handicapping strategies are as well as your red flags. You have poor perspective because you live inside the frame. To prevent this, ask your friends what your red flags are (e.g., what gets you upset easily, and what obstacles do you purposely set). This information will bring important awareness to what is blocking you from hearing your Lifesong.

CHAPTER 4

FLIP THE SWITCH

"There is no such thing as bad weather, only bad clothing."

— a Nordic saying

IN A NATIVE-AMERICAN PROVERB, A FATHER TELLS HIS SON ABOUT THE BATTLE THAT GOES ON INSIDE EVERYONE'S HEAD. The father says, "My son, the battle is between two wolves inside us all. One is weak. It is jealousy, distraction, sorrow, regret, arrogance, inferiority, fear, and self-pity. The other is strong. It is joy, love, hope, focus, kindness, compassion, confidence, and peace of mind."

The son thinks about it for a minute and then asks his father, "Which wolf wins?" The father simply replies, "The one you feed."

Unfortunately, many individuals have made it a bad habit to continually feed their "weak" wolf. When adversity arrives at their doorstep, they begin to pout and turn bitter. They see the world in a morose light and easily tumble down the rabbit hole of darkness. This "weak" wolf then grows and grows until it is out of control and has taken over their lives.

Other people, however, choose to feed their "strong" wolf. When times get tough, and the world seems against them, they flip the switch to see their life difficulty as an opportunity for growth. They choose to see all the positives in a troubled situation. Because of this attitude, they rebound much more easily from a terrible turn of events. Their "strong" wolf allows them to lead a productive and fulfilled life, regardless of circumstance.

Which wolf do you typically choose to feed?

Willie Mays, one of the all-time baseball greats, always chose to feed his "strong" wolf. Mays is known for his great attitude along with his immense talent he had on the ball field. A former teammate recalled how one day at the start of a big game, Mays declared to the guys, "This is going to be a great day; I'm going four for four. No doubt about it." Mays then went to the plate and readily struck out looking. He came back to the dugout and told his teammates, "Today is a great day: I'm going three for four." When he failed to get a hit next time up, he then proclaimed to his teammates that he was going two for four that day. Then he grounded out to third on his next at bat and proceeded to the dugout telling whoever would listen that he was going one for four on this glorious day. Later in the game, when he was robbed of a base hit on his last at bat, he smiled and told his teammates, "Tomorrow is going to be a great day. I'm going four for four!"

Mays became one of the greatest ballplayers the sport has ever seen because he always chose to *flip the switch* and possess a positive outlook about his circumstances. Mays was following the eternal wisdom that Ohna shared with us in the parable—you always have the power to choose your attitude and move toward transcend-ability.

You are not different from Willie Mays. Regardless of the situation, you, too, have that same power. When life deals you a tough setback, you really have only three choices that will impact you and your surroundings. You can see the adversity in a negative light and play the victim of the tragedy. Second, you can view that tragedy as a nonevent and disregard it. Or third and your best choice, you have the power to see your hardship in a positive light—as an extraordinary project—as an opportunity to fall up.

In my research with individuals who turned their tragedy into transcendence, I discovered that their **second stage to achieve transcend-ability was that they flipped the switch** to see that their hardship had significant meaning. They came to the realization that this painful event is a special opportunity for personal growth. People with transcend-ability feed their strong wolf and this choice propels them to greater heights. Such is the true life story of Kia Scherr.

While in India on a family trip in 2008, Kia Scherr experienced a terrible tragedy. However, Kia used this experience as a catapult for personal growth. On this horrific day, a group of Mumbai terrorists attacked a café where her daughter and husband were eating. Both perished in that attack, along with hundreds of other innocent souls.

Kia told me that a big piece of herself died in that attack. She felt extreme loneliness for a long time. As a result of her loss, she completely turned off and disconnected from the world. At this point in her life, her heart was frozen in stone.

Then Kia made an impactful choice and decided to **flip the switch**. She chose to forgive the people who killed her family. She also chose to get reconnected with the world. Kia wanted this tragedy to have meaning and to share its message with the world. To accomplish this, she developed the One Life Alliance Foundation, which develops practical ways to build peace, particularly in India. The One Life Alliance helps to create pillars of peace by making wealth and education more equitable. Her tragedy is helping so many others because Kia chose to "Be the love you seek"—she chose love instead of hate. (Please see more about this foundation at onelifealliance.org).

Lawrence Humphrey is another phenomenal person who flipped the switch and transcended from the darkness to the light. He chose life instead of death, literally and figuratively. The sadness of Lawrence's story is that it happens all too often. He came from a very difficult childhood and had parents who were unloving and uninvolved. Worse yet, his father and role model was a drug user. Lawrence, in turn, went down that same path. He became a drug user and was continually in and out of rehab and jail for years.

Then Lawrence had a moment of pure awareness. While in a stint in rehab, he saw the light—he saw his destiny. He realized that if he were to continue on this path, he was going to end up dead in the near future. Lawrence told me that was the essential slap he needed to awaken from his dark sleep.

Fortunately, Lawrence had the strength to flip the switch as well as the courage to choose an alternate attitude about his life. In my interview with him, Lawrence told me that instead of playing the victim, he chose a future-oriented attitude. He became dedicated to making a new life for himself. Instead of focusing on the time he lost, he chose to focus on his precious moments that he had left. He began to cherish his life and let other people help him. As I write this, Lawrence is finishing up a bachelor's degree. His plan is to become a minister so that he can help people get their lives back on track, as he did.

While Kia and Lawrence are current examples of the second stage of transcend-ability, if you look closely, our history books are filled with many wonderful examples. An inspirational classic is the life history of Victor Frankl.

During World War II, Frankl found himself under the sadistic oppression of the Nazi regime. Being Jewish, his family was sentenced to a concentration camp. There, the Nazis killed his wife and unborn child, as well as his mother and father. He survived only by digging ditches for the dead and being a slave to the whims of his oppressor.

Frankl was subjected to horrors beyond what a human being should ever see and experience. But from his tragedy, he experienced an enlightenment of immense proportion. He saw that certain individuals, who were in the same situation as him, would give up hope, wither away, and die. Other people in the same situation, however, stayed hopeful and withstood the tortures of their oppressors; they lived to see their freedom.

From these experiences, Frankl wrote his seminal book, *Man's Search for Meaning*, and he developed a counseling philosophy called Logotherapy. There are three main tenets of Logotherapy. First, we have the freedom to choose how we view our conditions. This freedom actively shapes our lives and is essential to the human condition. The second tenet is that we must have meaning in our lives. Without meaning, individuals will experience an increase in psychological maladies and neurotic disorders. Third, the meaning in our lives is an objective reality. Everyone can find meaning from every situation with the appropriate attitude.

Ultimately, the wisdom of Victor Frankl is that you can view your hardship in any reality you choose. To exemplify this philosophy, Frankl stated, "The last of the human freedoms is to choose one's attitude in any given circumstance." Frankl showed us that regardless of event, **you have the power to flip the switch** and adopt a positive attitude about your life. This is your ultimate power. You always have the power to fall up!

Ralph Waldo Emerson, author and philosopher in the mid-nineteenth century, once said that you must not be the slave of your own past. All your thoughts, emotions, and energies can easily get stuck back in time to your tragedy. When that occurs, you can never move forward in your life unless you choose to let it go. Ultimately, flipping the switch is your willingness to let go of the tragic moment. When this occurs, the tragedy can give you greater self-respect and move you to a higher level of happiness. Choosing the right attitude will allow you to acquire transcend-ability and become your true self. Here are some powerful activities to help you flip the switch and move toward the light:

1. Get TUF.

Science has shown that those individuals who are super-resilient will view their hardships using a specific framework. It all starts with a simple awareness question—when people have a difficult life situation, a serious loss, or stinging adversity, they will want to know "why" this happened. Psychologists call these explanations for the "why" question *attributions*. Psychologists have also determined that the type of attributions a person uses will directly impact their level of resiliency.

More specifically, the most resilient individuals use "TUF" explanations. Ultimately the "TUF" strategy makes you believe that the terrible or failed event will change into a more positive event in the near future. Therefore, the "TUF" attitude bolsters your optimism and hope as well as enhances your motivation and commitment toward your goals. (Although modified, this process is based upon the work of Dr. Martin Seligman.)

The following is an example of the "TUF" attributional style:

1. The *T* stands for believing your adversity is *Temporary*. You tell yourself that such a failure usually never happens to you. It was a fluke occurrence. The focus of this attribution is that you believe that the failure or life difficulty is not permanent—only temporary. As an example, you failed the first chapter test

in your math class, but you believe that was just a temporary lapse in test taking. You will get your mojo back on the remaining chapters, and you will not fail any more tests.

2. The *U* stands for believing your adversity is *Unique*. This failure happened only for this one particular situation. You believe that this adversity will not happen across all situations. As an example, you failed the first chapter test in your math class. You tell yourself that you just didn't get that one particular subject in that chapter, but you will do well on subsequent math tests because you will get those topics.

3. The *F* stands for believing your adversity is *Flexible*. Flexible implies controllable factors such as effort and strategy. You believe that if you change your strategy (something within your control), then this adverse condition will not happen again. As an example, you believe that if you change your strategy, such as to get a math tutor going forward, you will begin to pass the remaining tests in your math class.

Ultimately, when you use the "TUF" mentality, you believe that negative events are fleeting, and more importantly, positive events are around the corner. This helps you possess a good attitude about the future and let go of the past. The good news is that you can flip the switch and choose a "TUF" mentality for any life situation. When this happens, you will supercharge your resiliency.

2. Develop a growth mindset.

In many cases, a stinging failure and a painful setback are essential feedback moments, and it is this feedback that will allow you to become the person you are meant to be. Such a moment changed the life of one of our most revered authors, Harper Lee. When Harper sold her first manuscript, *Set a Watchman*, the publisher thought it was disjointed and not fully developed. But it had potential. The publisher recommended to Harper to tell the story from the perspective of twenty years earlier, when Scout was a child.

At that moment in her life, Harper could have taken that pain of rejection and withdrawn her manuscript as well as herself from a literary life. She could have believed that the publisher was incompetent and did not understand her vision as an artist. But instead, she listened and incorporated that new viewpoint into a new story. It took another two years of hard work, but it was well worth the wait. Harper Lee's new book, *To Kill a Mockingbird*, became an instant bestseller and a modern-day masterpiece, and placed her on top of the pinnacle of the greatest American writers.

Constructive criticism is painful. It stings as it pierces your ego and makes you doubt your abilities. In many ways, a painful failure is constructive criticism for you to develop and move in a new direction. What is painful is essential to your growth.

When you receive criticism or a stinging suggestion, do you embrace it as an opportunity for growth or blow it off because it is too painful?

In her groundbreaking book, *Mindset*, Carol Dweck speaks about the importance of a growth mindset. Put simply, people with a growth mindset see criticism as positive fuel to achieve their potential. Individuals who possess a growth mindset evaluate success based upon improvement and whether or not they have personal growth from their experiences. That is, people with a growth mindset will have positive emotions and see themselves as successful if they are getting better at a chosen task or situation. Most importantly, as compared to their peer group, individuals who have a mastery mindset are happier, have greater motivation, and ultimately, lead a more successful life. It is obvious now that Harper Lee had a growth mindset.

People with transcend-ability have chosen a growth mindset. They make the choice to see everything as a blessing and as an opportunity for growth. Here are a few tips to develop a growth mindset about any life difficulty:

List three hardships in your life that caused you pain and torment:

_____

_____

_____

Describe how each difficulty has helped with your personal growth:

_____

_____

_____

Flip the switch and adopt the mindset that your hardships can always enhance your growth as a person.

Once you do this activity, you will begin to connect the dots and see that your life experiences create a purposeful picture.

3. Believing is seeing.

Our belief system can change our physiology. Medical research has documented time and time again how patients feel better when given an inert substance such as a sugar pill—if they are told that this pill will be beneficial to their health. They believe in the pill and it helps their healing process.

One recent powerful example of this "placebo effect" happened in surgery with athletes. When athletes get a tear in their knee cartilage, there usually is a need for surgery and then a long rehab process. In one fascinating study, a group of athletes had actual surgery on their tear. Another group of athletes with a tear were given a mock surgery. The doctor left a small mark on the leg making the participants in this group believe they had the same surgery as the first group. Amazingly, both groups healed at about the same rate. Our attitude can greatly affect our healing.

This placebo effect shows us the power of belief. You must flip the switch and believe that you can bounce back higher from your adversity. But you must believe it to see it.

4. Choose to release the hot coal.

A few years back at a conference, Rabbi Harold Kushner, author of the international best seller *When Bad Things Happen to Good People,* told the audience an impactful and insightful story about why we must let go of our pain and ultimately forgive. He spoke of a woman who had immense hatred for her ex-husband. He had left her alone to take care of the children, along with the bills, all while he traveled the world with his new girlfriend.

Rabbi Kushner related that it was as if she were holding a hot coal in her hand. She was waiting for him to come back, so she could throw it at her ex-husband's face. But poignantly, Kushner emphasized that the coal was only burning her. The hatred she felt for her husband was causing her to be imprisoned in her pain. The hatred was only burning her from the inside out and destroying her happiness.

Kushner then told her that she must forgive him, and in doing so, it would release that hot coal from her hand and heart. Forgiveness would be an act of self-love and free her from the bonds of her hatred. Kushner told her to write what would be a very difficult forgiveness letter. She never had to mail it to him, but she had to write it.

To let go and move on, you must choose to release the hot coal inside of you. You must choose to let go of the past, and ultimately the pain. As Kushner suggested, first write a letter stating how this person or situation impacted your life. But most importantly, express your forgiveness. You can send it (if it is a person who caused your hardship), or just keep it, but you must write it to move forward. With this letter, you are choosing the path toward your transcend-ability.

5. Snap the rubber band.

Let's be honest. It is easy to fall into the negativity viewpoint. It is difficult to let go of that hardship that changed your life. It is easy to ruminate continuously about this event so that it creates poison in your brain. It is easy to develop a negative habit about your tragic moment.

The rubber-band technique is very effective for switching off the negative mindset and switching on a positive outlook. First, place a rubber band around your wrist. Next, every time you find the tragic moment taking you to a darker place, snap the rubber band. Not so much that it hurts, but rather it gets your attention. Then, replace that negative thought with a positive thought about how this adversity has made you a better person (or some similar thought).

Over time you will discover that your negativity toward this difficult moment diminishes. If you want, you can keep the rubber band on your wrist as a reminder to always make the right choice.

6. Create a best friend journal.

Besides getting rid of your negative thoughts, you can talk yourself into a better attitude. This principle is called self-talk. It is an extremely powerful tool to flip the switch in times of need. Take the amazing story of Billy Mills.

A Native American who was orphaned at the age of twelve, Billy Mills grew up on a reservation. Eventually, he won an athletic scholarship to the University of Kansas, where he helped his track team win two national championships. After graduation, he joined the marines.

While in the marines he trained himself to rise to the occasion. He had planned to run the 10,000-meter race in the 1964 Olympic Games, and used self-talk as his key strength. Every day he would write positive self-statements in his "best friend" journal such as, "You are going to have a great kick in Tokyo" and "You will have great positive energy at the Olympics." It worked like magic.

As Billy was coming around the last lap in the Olympic finals, he was in third and said to himself, "Third is okay." Staying in third would have been the easy choice for Billy. But something inside changed and Billy flipped the switch. Billy began to say to himself, "I can win, I can win, I can win." With those words, he produced an incredible burst of energy and had one of the greatest final kicks in Olympic history. Billy Mills passed the two competitors in front of him in the final twenty meters, putting him atop the podium after the race, holding his gold medal.

You can be like Billy. With the right words, you can flip the switch and choose an attitude that allows you to overcome adversity. The first step is to create your own best friend journal. Every day in your journal, write a positive self-statement such as, "Keep up the fight" or "You are a life champion!" Then state this phrase over and over again to instill a habit of positive self-talk. The right words at the right time will be a powerful mental weapon to creating the life you want.

7. Be like Bruce Lee.

Bruce Lee, the famous martial artist and actor, used a powerful technique to flip the switch. When negative thoughts would enter his mind, he would write those unwanted thoughts on a piece of paper. Then he would take the piece of paper, wad it into a ball, and throw it in the trash can. Then he would visualize the paper catching fire in the trash can. Once destroyed, those specific negative thoughts would never again enter his mind.

Be like Bruce—do not let negative thoughts control your happiness. Knock them right out of your mind.

8. Get the irony out.

Please don't think of a pink elephant. Please don't think of a pink elephant.

So, what did you just think about?

What else but a pink elephant! Psychologists relate this phenomenon to the ironic-process theory. By telling yourself not to think about something, it will actually force your thoughts in the unwanted direction. Thus, the irony.

This same principle will go for your thoughts about your tragedy or adversity. When you think about how this situation has caused you pain or discomfort, all your energy is focused on the negative. Your thoughts keep you stuck in that unwanted direction.

Become less ironic in your life. Reframe your thoughts and self-talk toward where you want to go in life, and not what you are trying to avoid. Focusing all your energy in the desired direction results in moving in that direction. How ironic you did not think of all this before!

10. Choose laughter.

When the pressure of life builds up, and you feel like your life's difficulties are taking you down the rabbit hole of negativity and depression, you might just need a release mechanism. The great thinker and writer William Shakespeare believed in the power of a release mechanism when he wrote, "They laugh that win." Shakespeare was referring to those who can laugh their sorrows away as doing themselves a great service.

Laughter can be one of the best antidotes to our difficult times. Besides just being a physical release, researchers have shown that laughter releases hormones known as endorphins that are considered the brain's natural opiates, giving you a sense of euphoria. In essence, laughter can make you feel good even during a sour time.

Also pertinent to this discussion is the work of Norman Cousins. In his groundbreaking book *Anatomy of an Illness*, Cousins described how he recovered from a debilitating illness by watching a variety of comedy shows and laughing himself to better health.

The choice is simple. You can get angry or sad when you think how life has given you a bag of rotten apples. In this case, you will probably ruin your days as well as your health. Or you can laugh at the difficult situation and tough times that you face. In this case, you will have a much sunnier day as well as much better health.

11. Enjoy the challenge.

The Greek mythological story of Sisyphus illustrates how to transform any adversity into an enjoyable challenge. Sisyphus was caught eavesdropping on the gods, and they became very upset with this type of mortal behavior. As punishment, the gods decreed that Sisyphus for all eternity would have to push a large rock up a steep hill until he reached the top. Sisyphus could never reach the top because the weight of the rock would overcome him, and it would roll back down the hill. Then he would perpetually begin the process all over again.

Except, Sisyphus was highly intelligent. He flipped his internal switch and decided that if he were to enjoy this eternal challenge, it would not be emotionally or physically painful. One time he rolled the rock as fast as he could, another time as slow. One time with his right hand and another time with his left, and he did this process over and over and over again. By implementing this strategy, he turned his painful situation into a joyous one.

Mihaly Csikszentmihaly, a famed psychologist and author of *Flow*, once stated, "Of all the virtues we can learn, no trait is more useful and more essential for survival than the quality to transform our adversities into an enjoyable challenge." Be like Sisyphus and flip the switch to enjoy the challenge of overcoming your struggles.

12. Let it be.

Accepting your situation is another way to flip the switch. Take this remarkable true story of a Beatle legend. While Paul McCartney had many career highs, much of 1968 was not one of them. The Beatles' stint together was winding down and the breakup of the band was looming. Single at the time, he was staying up too late, drinking, clubbing, and, as he put it, "wasting my life away."

One night, however, changed all of that. During a dream, his mother Mary appeared. She had died when Paul was only fourteen and he could barely remember her face. But in this dream, her face appeared crystal clear, particularly her eyes. She said only three words to him in a gentle, reassuring voice, "Let it be."

McCartney awoke with a great feeling. He felt his mother had given him a message he desperately needed: It would all work out and he should stop resisting the downturn and just let it be.

Soon after waking, he went to the piano and started singing the now famous lyrics, "When I find myself in times of trouble, Mother Mary comes to me, speaking words of wisdom. Let it be."

Apply the "Let it Be" philosophy to your life. Life is a roller coaster of ups and downs. Accept the inevitable bad breaks that come with life. When they occur, and they will, know that life will eventually switch directions. Your downward spiral will eventually stop, and you will begin an uphill path. Let it be like Paul McCartney, and this mentality will give you the peace of mind that your life will get better.

13. Choose to live in a friendly universe.

Albert Einstein once stated that to be happy, you must ask yourself, "Do I live in a friendly universe or a hostile one?"

What universe do you typically choose?

If it is a friendly universe, then you believe everything happens for a reason to help you. With this perspective, you believe the future will work in your favor. You will have a sense of calmness and peace, regardless of the situation or difficulty. You just accept all circumstances as learning situations. In direct contrast, when you believe the universe is hostile and against you, then you will always be filled with anxiety and frustration when life does not go as planned.

As Victor Frankl told us many years ago, you have the freedom to choose your universal perspective. Making the wise choice will lead to your happiness and a life of transcendence.

CHAPTER 5

RELEASE YOUR GENIUS

**"Everyone is broken by life, but afterward
many are strong in the broken places."**
— Ernest Hemingway

PICTURE A BRIGHT PLUMP ORANGE. Now let me ask you three simple questions:

Question 1: If I squeeze this orange, what comes out?
Answer: Orange juice. (This is not a trick question.)

Question 2: Why does orange juice come out?
Answer: Because that is what's inside. Grapefruit or apple juice would never come out.

Question 3: What life juice have you put inside?
Answer: If you put in fear, negativity, and anxiety, then that is what will come out when you get squeezed. And you will get squeezed because that is the human experience. But if you put in positive life juice such as joy, compassion, and serenity, then those positive emotions will come out when you get squeezed.

When serious hardship, adversity, and tragedy put the **squeeze on you, your best self can emerge. The third stage of transcend-ability—release your genius—is when your true strengths, which have lied dormant, now appear when life squeezes you.** As illustrated earlier in the parable, Annie discovered she had great inner strengths of fortitude and commitment when faced with the evil in her company.

This third stage of transcend-ability has been illustrated wonderfully by one of the most beloved presidents in American history: Franklin Delano Roosevelt. When FDR got the squeeze from his physical hardships, his leadership genius flowed, which helped us get through two of the darkest times in history—the Great Depression and World War II.

But life did not start out difficult for Franklin. In fact, his early years were filled with much silver in his spoon. He grew up in beautiful and idyllic Hyde Park in New York state overlooking the Hudson River. FDR went to the best prep schools, eventually ending up at prestigious Harvard University and then attending Columbia Law School. He was given everything that a person of wealth could get, except a perspective for those born less fortunate—those with wooden spoons. That all changed in his thirty-ninth year.

At first, the doctors did not know what was wrong with Franklin. He had a high fever and his muscles became immobilized, so he was bedridden. Eventually, the diagnosis was grim. He had contracted polio. More piercing was that polio took away his once-powerful legs. From that moment forward, Franklin wore braces for support, always needing a helping hand as he shuffled his feet forward, never again able to walk by himself.

American inspirational author Orison Marden once wrote, "Deep within humans dwell those slumbering powers: powers that would astonish them, that they never dreamed of possessing;

forces that would revolutionize their lives if aroused and put into action." Those words epitomize the life of FDR. His experience with polio forced dormant forces to come alive under extraordinary circumstances.

While polio took away his physical prowess, it unleashed strengths and **released his genius** that FDR would use throughout his presidency. In the past, his well-known name and charm created an easy walk to the top of the political ladder. His polio, however, forced him to take the path less traveled. His difficult and unsuccessful recovery to walk on his own merit had taught him that he must work for everything. From then on, nothing was given easily. Everything he was going to achieve had to be won with a battle. But those tough times had sparked his fighting spirit to come alive. His true life juices were awakened.

Even more vital to his political ingenuity was his empathetic development. He went from a self-absorbed rich kid to an empathetic politician who cared about the common man. And unlike his predecessor, Herbert Hoover, he now could relate to all types of loss and despair. The plight of the masses during the depression hit him deeply. He could feel their pain and so he was determined to act. And act with vigor he did. In his New Deal initiatives, FDR spearheaded some of the most far-reaching legislation this country had ever seen. He created a variety of programs that produced relief for the unemployed, created economic growth, and developed financial reform so that any future economic crisis would be minimized.

His physical hardship propelled him to become the president the country desperately needed during an extraordinary time. Throughout his presidency, his polio helped him to deeply connect and build essential trust with the American people at a level that never would have been achieved without his personal tragedy. At his funeral procession, the story is told that a man began to kneel down and weep. His friend asked if he knew the great president. He replied: "No, but he knew me."

FDR is not an anomaly of human nature. Rather, history is lined with people who have garnered essential strengths from their despair. While much has been written about the genius of Albert Einstein, less voice is given to how his early tragedies focused his immense intellect in solving one of the most important physics problems of all time. First, Einstein suffered a painful breakup with his first wife, Maleeva. She went back to Zurich with their two children and left him in Berlin, alone and heartbroken. Second, all his colleagues as well as his friends were in complete support of his country, Germany, to fight in World War I. They all believed it was right and morally acceptable for Germany to fight in this war. Einstein, on the other hand, was an active pacifist who protested the war as well as wore the banner of a war resister in all his discussions. As a result, he was shunned by his colleagues and rejected by his working inner circle. His friends and colleagues disowned him. At this time in his life, Einstein became isolated and cut off from his world.

While extremely painful, these moments were quite beneficial: they forced Einstein to immerse himself into his science and **release his genius**. He began to take another look at the mathematics of his new physics framework, what became known as the General Theory of Relativity. As a result, he realized his earlier mathematics were wrong in terms of his calculations for the bending of light by the forces of gravity—one of the key principles in his new theory. With this error, no outside scientists would have been able to prove his revolutionary ideas. He would have been discredited, and his theory would have been seen as worthless.

But history tells us that his pain of loneliness supercharged Einstein's strength of focus and created a universal perspective of physics not known until he discovered it. He corrected his theory, and this allowed other great minds in physics to see the light and support his ideas. Without his painful personal hardships, Einstein would have been only a footnote in space and time.

But such historical stories of transcendence are not just reserved within books in the library. It does not matter if you are a famous leader or scientist. Today, everywhere you look, you will find individuals who found their genius because of a serious hardship. Take the amazing life story of Gil Battle.

Battle had gone to prison for forging checks to feed his drug addiction. He only survived, both mentally and physically, because of his tattooing talents. Gil would make amazingly artistic tattoos for prisoners, and in turn they would protect him from any harm.

When he was released from prison, Gil began to use his new talent, but instead of arms and legs, he began to tattoo ostrich eggs. Gil was fascinated with how beautiful an ostrich egg could become under his watchful eye. More importantly, his younger brother told him to use his stories in prison as themes on his egg art.

Together, Gil and his eggs became magical. He began to turn his eggs into what looked like the famed Fabergé eggs of days gone by. But instead of their being ornamented with diamonds and rubies, he designed his eggs with fascinating stories about chain gangs or abused boys who then abused the world. Gil tattooed his eggs with all the fear, hatred, and hardships that he experienced in prison. Those painful stories on his ostrich eggs are now showcased in galleries around the world and sell for as much as $14,000 each.

Without prison, Gil would be lost in time and direction. His hardship **released his genius** and shone a light on his true path. As his son described it, "My dad's time in prison unleashed his true talents, and now he can share his true genius with the world."

In the middle of crisis, comes clarity. When we allow it, chaos can focus the mind as a sharp penetrating arrow that propels us in the right direction. Life difficulties created the clarity for Joel Bunkowske and propelled him toward his dream life.

Joel Bunkowske came to Nashville to build a music and entertainment company. He was creating exciting television shows as well as producing amazing music for talented artists. His goal was to create an MTV type of channel on the internet. People began to take notice of his work, and soon his company was worth $30 million.

With all that newfound money, Joel began to live the high life. He travelled to exotic places and bought nice cars and a beautiful home. Then the dot-com bubble burst, torpedoing his company. His economic world had flipped. He lost everything. Soon, Joel found himself on the verge of bankruptcy. His home was about to be foreclosed and he was trying to keep his family from going homeless. As Joel explained to me in our discussions, "I got down on my knees and asked God for a direction."

Looking in the want ads, Joel found a legal opportunity to work on wills and trusts. (He is a lawyer by trade.) At the interview, Joel was told about another opportunity to speak in front of the top brass for a Ford division in Chicago. Joel took the ultimate risk and flew to the Windy City on his last dime, hoping his luck would change direction.

Joel told me that at that moment he had a wake-up call. While speaking under the intense spotlight with everything to lose, he **released his genius**. As Joel states, "It was magical. My words flowed from me with an intensity that I never before experienced." His audience was captivated by his every word. Until that moment, he had not realized he was a terrific speaker. The top brass hired him on the spot, and he was on his way to a new path in life.

Joel discovered his new Lifesong. He eventually left the Ford company and became a full-time speaker for the Fred Pryor seminar company. He would travel the country sharing his knowledge about business and legal issues. Today, he uses his speaking skills as a successful professor at Devry University.

When one door closes, another one opens. Most people associate this piece of wisdom to the loss of a job or a relationship. But this human truth also applies inwardly. Tragedy can magnify your senses and connection with your world. For Jim Stevens, his loss of sight forced him to realize an amazing talent that was hidden from view.

While serving in Vietnam, Stevens had the misfortune to be standing in the path of enemy fire. He survived, but, unfortunately, shrapnel from a grenade got lodged in his head. Nevertheless, he came back from his war experience, got married, had children, and became a professor.

As time went by, however, the extra metal in his head took its toll. The shrapnel caused a severe stroke and, as a result, Jim lost his eyesight. Subsequently, his wife left him, leaving him alone to parent the children. And to make matters far worse, he left the job he loved. He felt the loss of sight would negatively affect his ability to teach his students.

Just like most people reacting to such a dark point in their lives, Jim grew extremely bitter toward the world. He told me that his two young girls began to incorporate his bad attitude, and this turned into severe behavioral problems for them at school.

Fortunately, Jim came across some material that explained how martial arts could help with school difficulties, so he enrolled his daughters. They agreed only if their father would attend the classes with them, for his daughters saw his need for enlightenment. Jim attended reluctantly, believing that a blind man would have a very difficult time learning a demanding physical skill like martial arts.

For the next three months, Jim just sat there and listened during class as his daughters participated. He listened to what his sensei was teaching. He listened to the movements of the other students. He listened to what footsteps really sounded like. He began to differentiate the subtleties in the sound between a kick and a punch.

His ears had now become his vision to the world and his greatest strength. In fact, Jim **released his genius** and discovered an inner strength he never imagined—**echolocation**. In echolocation, the object sends sound waves back to the person, and the person forms a picture in their mind. Like sonar, he could now envision the movement of others through sound.

Eventually, with his newly discovered strength, Jim gained immense confidence in his martial arts abilities. He stopped just listening. He began to participate and got really good at his new skill. Incredibly, at the age of fifty-one, Jim won a martial arts tournament of champions. Even more incredible, his competitors had no idea he was blind because he did not bring a cane into the ring. His competitors only realized he could not see after the event—to their shock, and to Jim's delight.

As an added bonus, his new ability to connect with the world helped Jim lose his bitterness. As he explained it, "I transformed into a better human being and a more compassionate person." He also regained his confidence in his artistic ability and began creating in earnest. Today, Jim Stevens is a renowned artist with works in galleries all over the world. He recently was honored for his work in the visual arts at the Kennedy Center in New York.

The new school of thought in psychology, known as "positive psychology," proposes a happier and more fulfilled life comes when you use your strengths on a daily basis. The next section of this chapter gives you strategies to **release your genius,** every day, in all areas of your life:

1. Your tragedy makes you unique.

Your tragedy is your uniqueness; no one else had the exact same experience that you did. Whether it is losing your sight or a loved one, your tragedy has allowed you to see the world with a new perspective—a unique perspective. This hardship experience gives you the advantage to perceive and interact with the world—in your own unique way. Your uniqueness is your ultimate strength.

2. Tragedy can magnify your strengths.

Science shows us that intense pressure can turn a worthless piece of coal into a magnificent diamond. The same principle goes for tragedy. The pressure of dealing with a tragic moment or serious life difficulty can supercharge your strengths and make you shine like a diamond.

This principle changed Bobbie C. from an average songwriter into a hit-making machine. As Bobbie C. told me, "I was just a run-of-the-mill songwriter until my loss." Bobbie lost his dear wife to cancer. It was extremely traumatic for both him and his three children. But as Bobbie put it, "This loss transformed me as a songwriter. I began to express emotions in my songs like never before and write lyrics at a deeper level that really connected to my audience. It was as if treasure dropped out of the sky on me. My songs took on a richer tone." While extremely tragic, Bobbie's loss thrust him into a higher stratosphere of songwriting. Today, Bobbie C. writes hit songs for many big-name performers and has been blessed with a remarkable career.

Your tragedies and life difficulties can magnify your magnificence. Go back and reevaluate some of your strengths. As Bobbie discovered, you might be surprised how your strengths have been supercharged to another level.

3. Hardships can boost self-confidence.

To Annika Sorenstam, it was the most intense spotlight she ever faced. Sorenstam, at the time the dominant woman player on the LPGA, competed with the men on the PGA Tour in 2003 at the Colonial tournament in Texas. Annika said the pressure was like all four majors rolled into one. She played great and missed the cut by only two strokes, but this event showed her that she could handle any level of pressure. This event supercharged her confidence, and she used it as a springboard to raise her game to a new level.

This same principle of pressure applies to you. There is much internal pressure from a severe hardship. There is pressure to move on with your life and not let the hardship pull you down into an emotional abyss. Be like Annika and allow this pressure of your tragedy to bolster your confidence. If you got through this terrible event, you could get through anything. Adversity can swing your resilience in the upward direction, if you let it.

4. Free your strengths by sharing.

Every fall, Austin Peay State University holds a "Clothesline" project. This project is designed to address violence and abuse. Participants decorate a shirt to express their traumatic experiences and then hang it up on a clothesline for all to see in front of the University Center. Some shirts might say: "Please stop hitting me, Daddy" or "Your words hurt." The shirts are very expressive and profound, and the project allows the participants to express their pain as well as bring a greater awareness to this serious societal problem.

Kelly (one of the participants) said that all the painful emotions flowed back into her heart when she sat down and wrote her painful words on the shirt. But, most importantly, she said that since making her shirt, she has gone through a powerful transformation. Kelly added, "It's the most amazing feeling in my life because this shirt started a process that freed me. It was the project that did it, and now I can tell my story." Today, Kelly has become an author and has written about her story for others to learn and grow.

Do your own clothesline project in which you place some of your feelings about your tragedy on a shirt. Hang it at your house or somewhere more public. Or perhaps you can simply begin a journal expressing your emotions about your hardship. You never know what strengths might rise out of the wash.

5. Drop the anchor of expectations to find your strengths.

Personal hardships come in many different colors and sizes. For Steve Jobs, a more contemporary artist of sorts, one of his personal tragedies came in the form of being fired from the company that he started—Apple Computers. But, according to him, it was "the best-tasting medicine for the patient" as it freed him from the pedestal of greatness. As Steve put it, he was the poster child for the new generation in the computer age, and those expectations were like shackles weighing him down personally and professionally. When he got fired, he felt that anchor of expectation had dropped, and he subsequently moved into one of his most creative periods.

Do you have expectations from others that are holding you back?

To drop the anchor of those expectations and free your strengths, do the following:

1. List the five main expectations that you believe others have of you.

_____

_____

_____

_____

_____

2. Next, explain how each expectation is holding you back.

_____

_____

_____

_____

_____

3. If those expectations were dropped, what strengths would appear? List one strength for each expectation.

_____

_____

_____

_____

_____

You don't need an event to free you from your expectations. It is within your power to drop the anchor of the expectations that others have of you. You have this freedom of choice.

6. Combine your strengths.

When you combine your strengths, you double your chances at being happier and more successful. This process worked for Mark McCormack, who started the famed sport agency, International Management Group (IMG).

Mark was a young lawyer and great negotiator as well as a good golfer and golf enthusiast. Through his many connections, he befriended the young Arnold Palmer and persuaded him that he (Mark) could manage all his business opportunities while he (Arnold) could focus on his golf. With only a handshake, Mark became Arnold's agent, and the sports agent industry was born.

While Mark would have been a very successful lawyer, when he combined his strengths, he doubled his level of success. To increase your happiness and success, first list your top five signature strengths. Better yet, take a strength assessment at www.authentichappiness.org. This assessment is called the VIA Survey of Character Strengths and it gives a listing of your twenty-four signature strengths.

Can you combine any of those strengths? Perhaps one of your strengths is creativity and another is being a great communicator. Can you combine those into doing seminars or writing a blog? Or one of your signature strengths is your golfing ability and another is communication. Perhaps you should go play golf with the boss. When playing golf, you will feel more comfortable talking to your boss because you are using both of your key strengths.

Create a plan using a combination of your strengths, and you can double your level of happiness and success.

7. Mold your talents like Matisse.

As many people know, Matisse is one of the greatest French impressionists. Walk into any museum in the world, and you will likely find a Matisse hanging on the wall for patrons to gaze upon with admiration.

Lessor known is the second act of Henri Matisse, when he placed scissors to paper. After suffering from a terrible illness called necrosis that left him bedridden, Matisse was forced to give up painting masterpieces. Immensely famous in his lifetime, he could have rested on his laurels and sat in his villa in the South of France and enjoyed a quiet retirement. But Matisse did no such thing.

Instead, Henri Matisse molded his immense art talent into another form—he began to do cutouts. Yes, just like the children at school who cut out paper silhouettes and plaster them on the walls in their classrooms. But of course, this was Matisse and his cutouts were like a majestic sculpture done by a master. Today, his cutouts are so admired that many museums exhibit his unique hand-cut artistry.

The life story of Henry Matisse teaches us many important lessons about how tragedy can mold your talents:

Lesson 1: Your talent will find you. Henri Matisse could not rest on his laurels because he had the need to continue his art. No tragedy would stand in the way of his talent. Your talents will find you—if you listen!

Lesson 2: Don't be afraid to change. It is very easy to get locked into your comfort box. Painting was the medium for Matisse, but he knew he had to change to allow his passion to stay free. Change is not fear-inducing to high achievers. Rather, you must see change as exhilarating. It all depends on your mindset.

Matisse once said that you should never be a prisoner of yourself, a prisoner of your style, or a prisoner of success. Let his life story allow your adversity to be the chisel that frees your true strengths.

CHAPTER 6

DISCOVER YOUR LIFESONG

**"When a person does not know what harbor
he is sailing for, no wind is the right wind."**

— Seneca (Ancient Greek philosopher)

D RIVING TO SPRING TRAINING IN FLORIDA, HALL OF FAME BASE-
BALL PLAYER AND MANAGER YOGI BERRA AND HIS WIFE WERE
TERRIBLY LATE. They were driving all night, and Yogi's wife fell fast
asleep. To make up for lost time, Yogi took a shortcut that eventually turned into a dirt road with more dirt than road. His wife
suddenly awoke, very startled, and said to Yogi, "Honey, I think
we're lost." Yogi, with all his pearls of wisdom, quipped, "Yeah,
but we're making great time."

Without discovering your **Lifesong**, you may get somewhere,
but most likely it will be the somewhere you don't want. Your Lifesong is your true path in life—it's your life's purpose. Living your
Lifesong is analogous to what Joseph Campbell called "following
your bliss." Your Lifesong has been there all the while, just waiting
for you to find it—and when you discover your Lifesong, an overwhelming sense of serenity takes hold of you, because now you

feel the universe is in complete alignment with your being. When the parable's Annie discovered her Lifesong, she transformed into a person of character and worth, and created a blissful life. **At this fourth stage of transcend-ability, you discover your Lifesong, and you begin to harmonize with your surroundings to become the person you were meant to be.**

The Light of the Lifesong

Your **Lifesong** is your inner light—the light that shines on your authentic self. We all need this light. In essence, this light is essential to our being. It is a survival mechanism. Psychologists discovered that when mice were placed in a tub with no way out, they would stop swimming after forty-five minutes and drown. However, if the mice had a light shining upon them, they would continue to swim for thirty-six hours. The mice were motivated through the darkness by a vision of light.

When Christopher Reeve found his **Lifesong**, it created the light that guided him through his most difficult times. Reeve's rise to fame came quickly in the 1970s with his portrayal of Superman in the movies. Then tragedy struck. During an equestrian competition, his horse threw him and he landed on his neck. His injury was so severe that he was paralyzed from the neck down. He could only breathe with a respirator.

But this terrible tragedy gave Christopher a new Lifesong—a new purpose to his life's direction. At his forty-third birthday party, he announced that he would stand up and make a toast at his fiftieth. To accomplish his vision, Christopher started a charity bearing his name with its goal to raise funds for spinal cord research. He circumvented the globe, giving countless speeches to inspire people to his quest.

Unfortunately, his vison was never realized. Sadder was his death at the age of fifty-two of a heart attack. But his story showed us how your Lifesong can give you that inner light and make you unstoppable.

Lifesong Promotes Courage

More than 150 years ago, Henry David Thoreau prophetically wrote, "Most men (people) lead lives of quiet desperation." Thoreau, one of the founding fathers of the self-help movement, captured the eternal human condition that persists to this day. Whether it is lack of determination or direction, most people do not achieve the life they had envisioned, but rather simply exist in resignation of their current situation. They give up on living a life of their dreams. They let their light go out.

Living your Lifesong is not easy. In many cases, becoming the person you were meant to be can be quite difficult. It can take immense courage to stop living in quiet desperation and move toward a life filled with joy and fulfillment. It takes great inner strength to admit you are not as happy as you want to be and to acknowledge you are not on your path. As Dottie Denis explained to me in our discussions, it took immense courage to move in a new direction and capture her true inner light.

Dottie grew up in a small rural town in the Deep South. Her formidable years were extremely painful. Her father was verbally abusive and always throwing negatives at Dottie. Her mother was very religious and believed that the woman's role is to stay home and have babies. At first, Dottie believed in this extremely traditional family viewpoint. Right out of college, she married a man who was similar to her father—abusive. Fortunately, this marriage did not last long. Unfortunately, she married another man who was an alcoholic and even more abusive than her first husband.

Given her upbringing, Dottie decided to stick it out and try to fix this relationship. Further, she felt immense guilt for letting her mother down in the first divorce. She did not want to do that again and be a double disappointment. But her marriage became more and more unbearable. As Dottie put it, "I was completely beaten up—emotionally and spiritually." She had reached the bottom of the bottom in her life. The darkness was pervasive.

Then, she awoke from her misery. Her young son, who had just enrolled in college, said to his mother these words of wisdom: "You look so depressed. Why don't you start college with me?"

Until this moment of enlightenment, Dottie was totally numb and completely unaware of the depths to which her despair had sunk. But even so, those comments by her son allowed her to flip the switch. Dottie decided that she needed some positives in her life—any positives would be wonderful. She knew she needed some pats on the back to stay alive emotionally. She needed a new direction in life.

Dottie gathered all her courage and started taking classes at the local community college. To her surprise, not only did she love college, but she was really good at all the courses. Dottie had no idea she had a particular strength for learning. She began to get the needed encouragement—her confidence grew and her spirit began to soar.

Eventually, she would earn her bachelor's degree, then a master's and then a PhD in the health field. She went on to become the dean of the graduate school at the university level. She is serving the academic world by helping other students attain the needed education for a better life. All her pain in life forged her path toward transcendence. Dottie now lives her Lifesong and has found her sweet spot in life.

The Flow of the Lifesong

When you are living your Lifesong, your positive energy will not only flow outward but also inward. Living your Lifesong will give you amazing contentment and joy. You are not concerned with achieving, but becoming. You are not forcing your life, but rather it feels effortless. When you live your Lifesong, the rhythm of a great universal symphony is heard from within.

A similar conceptual experience of living your Lifesong is being in flow. In the 1970s, Mihaly Csikszentmihalyi discovered that people do achieve a type of nirvana during a challenging activity. Flow is an optimal state of being in which your concentration is laserlike, your confidence overflows with abundance, and you feel immense joy in the moment. External rewards and outcomes do not matter; instead, the journey is the goal. In flow, you have endless positive energy.

Csikszentmihalyi discovered that flow can exist in a variety of venues. Athletes, musicians, artists, mathematicians, and business executives can all achieve a flow state. Anyone at any time can achieve flow. When people are in a challenging state but they believe they will meet those challenges with unbridled success, then a flow-producing state can be experienced.

There is, however, a key difference between the flow state and living your Lifesong. Flow is a temporary state. When it comes to flow, when the challenge is gone, so is the flow. A golfer will feel flow during the round—but not on the drive home. Flow only happens in a specific condition for a specific amount of time. In direct contrast, the Lifesong is a feeling of intense happiness that can happen every day, whether in a challenging situation or a calm one. Living in your Lifesong is living in a constant state of flow.

A tragic health condition caused Donny Anderson to harmonize with his surroundings and live in flow. At the young age of thirty-six, Donny had a massive stroke on the right side of his brain. It not only immobilized him physically but froze his spirit as well. All he wanted to do was to sit on the couch and do nothing. Donny's tragedy became a field of dark depression that encompassed his heart. Donny felt sorry for himself and turned that darkness inward by giving up on the world.

Then, one afternoon, he heard the crack of a bat coming from his back door. He went to investigate and found his destiny. Donny had always loved baseball and so from that day forth, he started to attend baseball practice every day at Arlington High School in Texas. He sat in his wheelchair watching the team practice—and the coach began to take notice of him as well. The head coach asked Donny to become his assistant, and that was like fueling a rocket ship. From then on, his spirit soared into the heavens.

Before his stroke, Donny was aimless and imprisoned with a lack of direction. He was a bartender, ambling through life in quiet desperation. He had no motivation to better himself. But now, because of his tragedy, he discovered the person he was always meant to be.

Living his Lifesong created a radical change in Donny. With much practice, he learned to walk again. He also enrolled in college as a special education teacher. Now he is in a constant state of joy, as he introduces children with special challenges to the Arlington baseball team, with everyone growing from this interaction, especially Donny.

The great philosopher and writer Albert Schweitzer once proclaimed, "The only ones among you who will be truly happy will be those who have sought and found how to serve." Donny lives this axiom and poignantly stated that he is thankful he had that stroke. This initial bitterness became an amazing betterment. He now has unbridled happiness because he makes a difference in the lives of others. His **Lifesong** sings and the world now hears it. Donny is the epitome of how to fall up.

For Christopher Reeve, Dottie Dennis, and Donny Anderson, their tragedies helped them to find the true rhythm of their lives. Unfortunately, most people are not in tune with what song really plays in their hearts. They do not harmonize with their surroundings, and they have no idea what path is true. **The good news is that you don't need a terrible loss or serious accident to discover your Lifesong.** All you need is essential knowledge as well as tools to guide your spirit. The following four-step process will help quiet all the noise and distractions so that you will begin to hear the rhythm of your Lifesong:

Step 1: Discover your purpose.

"What is your purpose in life?"

This is one of the most difficult questions you will ever have to answer, but the most essential. For Sandra Mulhinch, her purpose was discovered as a result of her husband's illness. Her husband has Amyotrophic Lateral Sclerosis (ALS), otherwise known as Lou Gehrig's disease, and his social worker told Sandra that he would die very shortly, so she needed for him to create his will. She felt upset and frustrated from that interaction and never wanted another person to feel that way when a loved one had a terminal illness. From this traumatic experience, Sandra told me that she realized her purpose was to become a clinical psychologist and work with families when a loved one suffers from a terminal illness.

However, many people don't know their purpose and so writing a purpose statement can be very difficult to many. To gain a clearer perspective, here are some essential questions to answer before writing down your purpose:

1. Who do you admire and why?
2. What have been some of the greatest contributions to our world?
3. What do you want to change in our world?

4. What significant contributions would you like to make to the world?

5. How do you want to be remembered?

First, answer these essential questions. Then reflect upon your answers. Your answers give clues to your true purpose. Now write two or three sentences that describe your purpose:

_____

_____

_____

_____

_____

_____

Step 2: Find your strengths.

In many cases, your strengths shine a light upon your true path. This happened to Stephen Garrett. By all measures, Stephen was living the American dream. He was a wealthy stockbroker who had the big car, the great house, travel—everything you could want in life. Then his sister, whom he adored, died suddenly of an illness. Stephen told me, "That event was like a slap in the face and shook me to my core. It was as if I was asleep at the wheel, but now was suddenly awakened to my unhappiness." His heart had cracked open and the immense pain of loss helped to shine a light upon his life.

Stephen flipped the switch, as he now knew that this terrible tragedy showed him that being a stockbroker was not his true path in life. Material wealth was no longer his primary objective in life. His sister's death was the force of change in his life—to become what he was destined to be.

Stephen's main strength is giving advice. He had developed that helping skill throughout his business life. Now Stephen transitioned his strengths as a money manager to a grief manager. He went from a counselor who focused on gaining more material wealth to a counselor who focused upon helping other people deal with their losses. In his loss, he gained a calling.

To help discover your Lifesong, list five of your signature strengths that you discovered in the previous chapter exercise, "Combine your strengths." If you did not take it yet, please do take the strength assessment at www.authentichappiness.org:

Signature Strength 1: _____

Signature Strength 2: _____

Signature Strength 3: _____

Signature Strength 4: _____

Signature Strength 5: _____

Step 3: Align your values.

Dr. Martin Luther King Jr. once said, "I do not want to have the finer things in life. All I want to leave behind is a committed life." King valued a life committed to the fight for human rights for all.

What do you value most? These might include civil rights, artistry, money, creating a useful product, helping the homeless, and/or making the environment better for our children.

List ten of your key values here:

_____

_____

_____

_____

_____

_____

_____

_____

_____

_____

Step 4: Discover your calling.

In the last part of this process, pick three different paths or callings that you might think are best for you:

_____

_____

_____

Now ask yourself which path aligns best with your purpose statement, your strengths, and your values. Be honest and thoughtful. The path that matches up best with these three key factors is most likely your true calling in life.

When you align your purpose statement, strengths, and values to your life path, your Lifesong will be heard loud and clear!

CHAPTER 7

MAKE 'PURPOSE' A VERB

"Be ashamed to die until you
have won some victory for humanity."
— Horace Mann (1796–1856), educator

"There are two types of people in the world—givers and
takers. The takers eat better but the givers sleep better."
— Danny Thomas, comedian
and founder of St. Jude Children's Hospital

DISCOVERING YOUR LIFESONG IS NOT ENOUGH. You must take action. **When you make *purpose* a verb, you have reached the final stage of transcend-ability.** At this stage, people move from a "me" orientation to a "we" orientation, with the focus upon making a meaningful impact in the world. As described in the parable, Annie Ainsworth made *purpose* a verb when she began to erect schools for impoverished children as well as created a foundation to develop a vaccination to eradicate the disease she had faced as a young girl.

The real-life story of Terry Fox is an amazing example of how to **make *purpose* a verb**. When Terry took action, he changed the consciousness of a nation. At the young age of twenty-two, Fox lost his leg to cancer. He was fitted with a prosthetic device so that he could walk without assistance. This experience awakened him to the devastation that cancer can have on your soul. This experience also awakened him to the ignorance that most people have about cancer. But most importantly, this experience awakened him to his true calling in life.

Fox designed an amazing Lifesong called "The Marathon of Hope." He would walk a marathon (26.2 miles) each day, with the ultimate goal of walking across the entire country of Canada, from the East Coast to the West Coast. His vision was to raise Canada's awareness about cancer, and his mission was to raise one dollar from every Canadian citizen toward cancer research.

Terry would walk twelve miles in the morning. Then he would take a break for lunch with his support team, which consisted of his best friend and brother. They did not walk with him, but followed him in a van. Then he would finish the Marathon of Hope in the afternoon.

It is amazing that someone could walk a marathon every day; but unthinkable that he could do that journey with a prosthetic device. But Terry could accomplish this unbelievable task because his Lifesong was filled with purpose, and purpose gives you a strength and energy that cannot be measured.

Although the Marathon of Hope started with a slight ripple of cheer, it ended with a tsunami of love. At first, no one knew of Terry's journey. But with help from the media, the entire nation of Canada got behind him and his Marathon of Hope. Canadians realized that Terry was serving his country's best interest, and so he gained their loving admiration. Thousands upon thousands began to cheer him on the streets as he passed or in stadiums when he stopped to speak about his purpose of eradicating cancer. The entire nation began to believe in him and his Lifesong. He was in the Canadian sweet spot.

Unfortunately, at the 3,000-mile mark, at Thunder Bay, Terry felt so sick that he had to stop the Marathon of Hope and be admitted to a hospital. He was devastated that he could not finish his Lifesong. But to his amazement, the country of Canada showed its support for Fox by creating an impromptu telethon during his hospital stay, raising $10 million for cancer research.

When you authentically connect with others by making a difference, the world will open its heart as the nation of Canada did for Terry Fox. While he never finished the Marathon of Hope—he succumbed to his cancer before he could complete it—his story did not fade in the hearts of his countrymen. Canada never forgot their hero. A statue was erected in his honor at Thunder Bay, with Terry Fox looking west to another journey.

The "Me" Mentality

The Marathon of Hope designed by Terry Fox was the epitome of the "we" mentality. Unfortunately, our culture does not promote the mentality that taking action and making a difference are essential qualities of a fruitful and desired life. Rather, the message we are typically bombarded with is the opposite—the promotion of the "me" mentality. Our culture continually reinforces the message that you should be the center of the universe.

This overemphasis on the self did not start with social media but has been around for generations. In the 1970s, famed author Tom Wolfe coined the term "the Me Decade" for that generation. He saw an explosion of a culture of narcissism. As he perceived it, this decade had become infatuated with itself. The concern of the decade was what others thought of you, as you always tried to stay in fashion and look your best. You were programmed to believe that being hip was essential and materials would fill any void.

Unfortunately, the internet has magnified the "me" mentality. Think "selfie." Recognized by the Oxford Dictionary as the word of the year for 2013, "selfie" is the dominant form in picture expression and perfectly captures the "me" mentality of our day. With an iPhone in every pocket, you can post your selfie to any one of your social media accounts in a heartbeat. Instead of taking a picture of a beautiful sunset at the beach, we "selfie" it by becoming the focus of attention with the beauty of nature as an afterthought.

The Problems with a "Me" Mentality

The "me" mentality creates the underpinnings for problems to our mental health. One of those underpinnings is fear, which directly relates to the adoption of a "me" mentality. We fear being inadequate, with the fear of "me" not living up to everyone else's standards. We fear looking incompetent and making mistakes. Most importantly, the fear of an inadequate "me" contributes to a higher level of anxiety and neurosis in your life, ultimately immobilizing you to take action as well as decreasing your success and happiness in every situation.

Fear can make you forget a speech and answers to a test. Fear can make you feel and sound stupid because the words jumble around in a mouth left dry. Fear can tighten up your muscles and make you choke during a sporting performance. When you are accompanied by fear, it is hard to live a life you always imagined.

In a related emotion, fear of not having enough can lead to selfishness—the namesake of "selfie." Selfishness is caused by a scarcity mentality, which is the belief that resources are scarce and there is only so much to go around. Thus, you must hoard and be selfish. With a scarcity mentality, you think, "I must get mine before you can get yours. I cannot help you to be successful because, if I do, I will not get mine." You believe that there are only so many sales to go around in your district and/or there are only so many clients who want to buy your product.

This scarcity mentality disconnects you from others. Your mantra is—"What's in it for me, and what can I get out of this relationship?" instead of "What can I give to the relationship?" It forces you to believe others can be a cheat and are out to take what is rightfully yours. This promotes feelings of isolation and aloneness. Instead of bonding with others in the chain of life—you act as one. You might be the center of the universe, but you are the only one in it!

But selfishness and fear are not the only negative emotions associated with a "me" mentality. There are plenty of other emotions that can destroy your happiness and mental health. Jealousy, envy, and resentment are pervasive when the focus is upon the self. When you compare yourself with others, you often don't live up to that comparison. Just look around. Turn on the television. There is always someone faster, smarter, richer, and better-looking. This thought process will lead to a life full of envy and jealousy. A focus on the self can only lead to a life filled with a sour taste in your mouth.

More radically, when envy, jealousy, and resentment are left unchecked, they will fester and become poisonous to the soul. In time, they can turn to hatred. Take the Bible story of Cain and Abel. As the ancient tale is written, Cain kills his brother Abel because of jealousy, envy, and ultimately, resentment. These emotions, and focus on the self, are timeless in their ability to make you suffer.

The Benefits to a "We" Mentality

Alternatively, making *purpose* a verb and having a meaningful impact upon others will give you immense inner strength as well as a life filled with sweetness and fulfillment. In addition, some scientists have suggested that the cooperative mode, and not the competitive mentality, provides you with the greatest advantage to survive. Biologist Lewis Thomas has stated that nature's law for all living things is not survival of the fittest where competition dominates, but rather cooperation rules the roost. According to Thomas, plants and animals survive not through competition, but by connecting and in cooperation, where each depends on the other to survive. The smallest species interacts with the largest species on our planet, and the only way to survive is through symbiosis. Take the example of bacteria in our saliva. The bacteria break down our food and help us digest our minerals and vitamins. The bacteria, in turn, live within us and we serve as their warm host. The "we" process of cooperation keeps us both alive and healthy.

In fact, we have remarkable benefits hardwired into our biology when we are in this cooperative mode of connection. When we make a positive social connection, the pleasure-inducing hormone, oxytocin, is released into our bloodstream, reducing anxiety and improving our ability to concentrate. Other research has shown that a positive connection with others can lower your blood pressure and decrease your chance for heart disease. Having a support system leads to less stress and a greater chance to overcome illness. In addition, the latest research in happiness shows that our personal connections are the primary ingredient for a satisfied and happy life.

Achieving transcend-ability is a loss of selfishness and jealousy and a move to an interconnectedness with others. Rather than possessing a scarcity mentality, individuals with transcend-ability have a plentiful mentality in which resources are bountiful, so that sharing is the mode of habit. Serenity and happiness come when you share yourself to make an impact in lives that need your help.

The life work of Craig Kielburger exemplifies these principles of transcend-ability at the highest level. **He found his sweet spot in life when he made *purpose* a verb and served others in need.** One morning at the breakfast table while in seventh grade, Craig opened the local newspaper and read a story that would forever change his life's direction. At that moment, he was awakened to the horrors around the world by a young boy, about Craig's age, named Iqbal Maish. The story explained that Iqbal was sold into slavery by his parents for less than sixteen dollars. For the next six years, he was chained to a carpet loom and forced to make carpets for twelve hours a day. The only food he was allowed to eat was a small bowl of rice and beans at the end of the day.

Iqbal then escaped his imprisonment to lead a crusade against such atrocities. He became an advocate informing his country of what terrible events were happening in the carpet world. Then one morning while riding his bike with other children near his home, Iqbal was shot to death. The police report stated that the assassin was hired by the carpet companies, and they were sending a clear message to all others who would speak against them.

That story flipped the switch deep inside the soul of Craig Kielburger. He knew he had to take action and make a difference in the lives of others. He vowed to continue the fight that Iqbal had started. At school that day, the young Kielburger told Iqbal's tragic story and asked the other students in the class if they wanted to help in the fight against these atrocities. Twelve hands were raised and the charity Free the Children was born. At that moment, Kielburger found his Lifesong.

The goal of Free the Children is to share with the world the horrors of child slavery; more importantly, it is to help eradicate this disgusting problem. Ultimately, this charity has a ripple effect because it is all about children helping children. Free the Children actively recruits children to show them how to make the world a better place. Besides building schools in impoverished areas, this charity sends children to summer leadership camp, which provides them with an enriched curriculum that expands their mind. Many of those children are sent on speaking tours to speak about the atrocities of children. Today, Free the Children (freethechildren.com) has grown into a $35 million charity with nearly two million children participating and growing stronger every day. This charity is the world's largest network of children helping children.

Kielburger knows the ultimate power of children. Poignantly, he stated that a child is analogous to a penny. People walk past them and many times ignore them, thinking they are insignificant. But when you bring enough young people together, then suddenly all those children have a rich impact on others. Craig shared that he was the happiest when he was bringing children together to make a difference in the world. Without a doubt, the world is a happier place with people such as Craig Kielburger.

Having an impact in the lives of others not only enhances our health and emotional well-being, it can also, literally, change our physiology. Take the life story of famed singer Carly Simon, who has such hits as "You're So Vain" and "Anticipation." Given her beautiful voice and wonderful singing career, it is quite surprising to learn that she grew up with a stutter. As a young child, she stuttered so severely that she never wanted to speak in public. Her stutter got so bad that she would avoid school out of embarrassment.

Intuitively, her mother said to Carly, "If you can start thinking about other people rather than yourself all the time, you may begin to lose your self-consciousness." Her mother knew that Carly was being too "me"-oriented and this was causing the stutter. She knew that her daughter could beat the torment of the stutter if she moved to a "we" mentality and began to focus on the needs of others.

When Carly made *purpose* a verb and developed a service mindset, her life radically changed for the better. She lost her selfish focus, and as a result, she lost her stutter and became one of the most popular girls in her class.

Thich Nhat Hanh, the author of *Peace Is Every Step,* knows the philosophic reason why Carly lost her stutter, writing, "The whole purpose of our lives is to overcome our sense that we are isolated, discrete individuals. We are here to awaken from our illusion of separateness." Nhat Hahn knows that our strength as a person comes when we think in terms of inclusion instead of exclusion. According to Nhat Hahn, "Like the water that carved out the Grand Canyon, one drop will not make a difference, but a stream of water can carve any rock." When Carly moved to a "we" mentality and authentically connected with others, she gained immense inner strength to overcome her stutter.

The cherished leader Mahatma Gandhi spoke often about the benefits to our well-being of a cooperative mentality: "The sweetest moments in life come when we are interconnected with others." People who achieve transcend-ability find a sense of peace and inner calmness when they turn their purpose into a verb and impact others. It happened to David Good.

At the tender age of seven, Good's life was turned upside down when his mother left the family. Years earlier, his father had met his mother, Yarma, while studying primitive cultures in South America. She came back to the United States to raise a family, but, over time, Yarma felt an urge to visit her homeland. She went home and never returned.

David never got over it. He completely rejected his mother and believed she had abandoned the family. More impactful, he was fearful that the other kids at school would find out who his mother really was and where she came from. All this anxiety was destroying David from the inside out.

His wake-up call came when David reached adulthood and read a book written by his father about his mother's tribe: the Yamani. Getting to know where she came from and her background allowed David to flip the switch in his mind. He could no longer run from his tragic situation. He knew he had to see his mother and ask her why she left. He had to face his tragic situation so that he could move forward in his life. He had to see his mother and the people in her village.

It took three difficult days of travel to reach the Yamani tribe. Two of those travel days were by small planes to isolated runways, with the final day in a canoe going up the rapids. But he finally reached the village. David and his mother reconnected instantly, as you would expect from a mother and son. More importantly, he connected with the Yamani tribe and saw how they lived and how they thrived in such an isolated world.

The biggest surprise came when David realized that this tribe did not experience loneliness or anxiety. They were an extremely close-knit group that relied on each other and were completely connected to one another. They were a symbiotic group, working together toward one unified goal. He saw that they were at peace because they have a special interconnectedness to survive. Their unity brings tranquility.

David realized how this unique tribe could help individuals be more mentally healthy and at peace with themselves—something he so desperately needed, and he knew others needed as well. **David made *purpose* a verb and launched the Good Project, a nonprofit organization that serves as a learning bridge between the Yamani tribe and the world.** David Good would fall up and find peace within himself when he made the world a better place.

One of our greatest thinkers, Albert Einstein, always believed in connection as the essence of life and most eloquently stated, "The separateness from others and the world around us is a delusion, and we must free ourselves from this prison by widening our circle of compassion to embrace all living creatures and the whole of nature in its beauty." The life theme of Terry Fox, Craig Kielburger, Carly Simon, and David Good (as well as all the other examples in this book) is virtually the same: We must not bury our heads to the problems and difficulties in ourselves as well as in others. We will not feel better about ourselves if we do. Rather, the more we shift our focus from personal gain to enriching the lives of others, the more empowered and fulfilled our lives will be. We must connect and embrace others into our circle. The more we give of ourselves to others, the more we get from the experience. **Your sweet spot in life arrives when you make *purpose* a verb by making a meaningful difference in your world.**

Best-selling author Rabbi Harold Kushner has stated, "One human being is no human being." We are meant to be interconnected. You can flip the switch and move from a "me" mentality to a "we" mentality. You can develop transcend-ability. It is more than possible; you have that power. Here are a few recommendations for making *purpose* a verb and moving toward an amazing life:

1. How may I serve you?

Someone who lived an honorable life that contributed much was famed self-help guru Wayne Dyer. The mantra for this inspirational guru was, "How may I serve you?" Because of this life philosophy, he achieved prosperity beyond his imagination and created a legacy beyond compare.

On the PBS television special, *I Can See Clearly Now,* Dr. Dyer recalls the story of how his agent got him an appointment with a high-profile publisher to discuss his latest book. To push the envelope, the agent reinforced how difficult it was to get this meeting, so Wayne needed to be at his best. As soon as the meeting started, he could see the publisher was distraught and distracted. Instead of talking about the book project, Wayne asked him about his problems and how he might help. (Wayne had a counseling psychology background, so he knew there was a problem.)

For the next three hours, all they did was talk about the issues bothering the publisher. Not once did they speak about the book during the meeting. The next day, Wayne called his agent and told him quite sheepishly how they never got a chance to discuss the book or its future with this publishing house. Needless to say, Wayne's agent was quite upset.

However, the next day that high-profile publisher called Wayne's agent and said that he did not get to discuss the manuscript, but that did not matter. His company was going to publish it anyway as he wanted to be in business with Dr. Dyer, a person of great integrity who cares about others.

Be like Wayne. Instead of thinking what can I get from this interaction, ask yourself: "How can I serve this person?"

With a change in this type of mindset comes happiness and success.

2. Service vs. fun

Sonja Lyubomirksy, author of *The How of Happiness,* discusses an activity which illustrates the power of service. The activity assesses whether your happiness increases more by doing acts of service or engaging in "just fun" activities. To see which one leads to greater happiness, do the following activity:

1. Create your own happiness scale from 1 to 10, with 1 being completely unhappy and 10 feeling completely ecstatic. Write a brief sentence next to each point on the scale according to how that happiness point feels to you. For instance, for point 1, you might write, "I am completely unmotivated and depressed" and for point 10, you might write, "I feel completely alive with hope."

2. For the first week, do one activity each day that you find "fun." This could be playing darts or golf or doing karaoke with friends. Then after the activity, rank your level of happiness on your scale.

3. For the second week, do one activity each day that is service-oriented. This activity is about placing the needs of others before your own. You can call your grandmother and tell her how much you love her or help someone with their groceries at the store. After this activity, rank your happiness on the scale.

4. At the end of these two weeks, look at your rankings and discover which type of activity led to your greater sense of happiness.

I do this exercise in my Happiness class. (Yes, I teach a class called "Happiness.") Every semester, the students discover what I hope you will find to be a human truth: When you act in ways of service, you are much happier and more fulfilled than when doing acts filled with just fun. Of course, you should continue both types of activities in your life. But service to others will always give you the greatest joy—so fill your life with the gift of giving!

3. Start a charity.

Kirk Douglas was the No. 1 box office movie star in the 1950s. In one of his movies, *Spartacus*, Kirk led a slave revolt against the Roman Empire. In real life, citizen Kirk led a revolt against the deplorable state of playgrounds in the Los Angeles area. More than thirty years ago, he and his wife saw the news story about the problems at these schools, and they wanted to make a difference.

Kirk started a foundation with the agreement that the LA Unified School District would match funds given by the Douglas Foundation. As of 2015, the foundation had opened more than four hundred playgrounds around the LA area, with Kirk usually the one to enjoy the first ride down the new slide.

Why did Kirk gain so much from giving?

According to him, it was simple: The act of giving rewarded him with an internal Academy Award. Kirk mentioned that he feels so good about giving to others, that he thinks it is selfish. He came to the realization that the act of giving is an amazing inner gift.

It might be easier to start a foundation when you are famous, but you don't need to be famous to start a charity you believe in. Just look around. There are thousands of charities started because those people who founded those charities turned their purpose into a verb. You can do the same!

4. Start a group that changes lives.

Jackie Turner had a childhood that was your worst nightmare. She never knew her mother and wished the same for her father because he would physically abuse her. When she was not being beaten, she was starved and neglected. Although those physical and emotional scars will forever be present, she made it through that dark period to become a college student.

Now that she's attending William Jessup University, the future is much brighter for Jackie. Getting good grades is the easy part. The difficulty comes when the holiday season approaches, when the dark clouds of depression roll into her life. Jackie has no one to share joy with during this cheerful season. She feels alone and isolated.

But Jackie took action to combat her loneliness and did something that would pull on anyone's heart strings. She created an ad on Craigslist, where she wrote, "I want to rent a mom and dad for a couple of hours." Furthermore, she added that the rented parents must act as if she was everything to them—their brightest light—and she would pay them eight dollars an hour to just sit there and talk. She wanted to rent a family for the holidays.

As you can imagine, Jackie got dozens of responses from parents who wanted to help—free of charge, of course. More amazingly, she got many more responses telling Jackie that they too felt the same as she did—alone and depressed during the holiday season. She found that there were many people just like her, hurting and broken, and in great need of a loving heart.

Instead of just focusing on her own needs, Jackie sweetened everyone's life with the power of a loving connection. She invited everyone who contacted her to attend a meeting, and she paired up the needy with the needed. The broken-hearted were paired with people who wanted/needed to share their love and compassion. She made sure no one was alone for the holidays that season.

You too can start a group that provides an interconnection, whether it is through Facebook or another social media channel. Jackie started a group that connected people in need and gained much from her efforts, and so will you.

5. Develop an attitude of gratitude.

About fifteen years ago, I learned the power of an attitude of gratitude and how it can have a powerful impact upon your happiness and success. A friend of mine was running the BellSouth Senior Classic golf tournament at Gaylord Springs Golf Links in Nashville. (This is the professional tour—and how it was named then—for players over fifty.) As a way to reach out to these players, I placed my golf psychology book, *MentalRules for Golf*, in every player's locker. I signed it with my name and contact info and a wish for good play that week. Only one player, Gary Player, called to thank me for the book.

To place this in perspective, Gary is a hall of famer who has won more than one hundred worldwide professional golf events. He is one of only a handful of professional golfers to win all four majors. Gary is a legend in the golf world, and he was clearly head and shoulders above the rest of the field that week in both fame and prestige. Yet, surprisingly, he was the only one to reach out to me with words of gratitude.

That event was my wake-up call to how important an attitude of gratitude is to your success. Gary is not all about the "me" mentality and winning. But clearly, he possesses a "we" mentality. He was thinking of others when he was giving me thanks for the book.

Also, this showed me that Gary possesses an attitude of gratitude. Being thankful allowed him to handle the bad breaks on the course as well as reduce his frustration when his game went south for the day. His attitude of gratitude helped him to stay calm and cool under pressure and, as a result, he played better in competition. He was thankful for whatever the game had in store for him, and this propelled him into the stratosphere of his profession.

Giving thanks and showing appreciation to others is simple yet very powerful. Like Gary Player, develop an attitude of gratitude to enhance your success and well-being.

6. Mastery vs. competitive attitude

The American way is to be the best. However, not all cultures value the premise of being number one as the ultimate goal. Some Eastern cultures value self-mastery as the mainstay for enlightenment. While being the best has its perks, a sole focus upon this objective can be detrimental to performance as well as your mental health.

Consider the parable of the American tourist who found himself in Japan on the day of a pilgrimage to the top of a sacred mountain. The tourist, who had been active all his life and in great shape, decided to join the pilgrimage. After twenty minutes, he was out of breath and could hardly climb another step, while elderly and the young villagers easily moved past him. "I don't understand it," he said to his Japanese companion. "How can all these villagers easily climb the mountain, yet it is so difficult for me?"

His friend answered, "You have the typical American attitude, and you see everything as a competition. You see the mountain as your enemy and you set out to conquer it. So, naturally the mountain fights back and wins. However, our culture does not see the mountain as our enemy, but a friend—a friend that will guide us along the way."

A competitive mindset is analogous to a "me" mentality. This type of mindset has a win/loss mentality. Someone must win and someone must lose, and it is the "me" that must win. More importantly, being in a competitive mindset is similar to a mountain always fighting against you. The pressure is immense to always be the best. There are a mountain of people trying to knock you off the top. In fact, researchers in psychology have shown that those individuals with only a competitive mindset have greater anxiety as well as lower motivation compared to those individuals with a self-mastery mindset.

To reduce anxiety and increase your inspiration, move away from basing your self-worth upon only competitive values. Instead, you should have a mindset that includes both self-improvement and competitive goals. Balancing your life with a variety of objectives will increase your chances for greater success.

7. Develop an abundance attitude.

A scarcity mentality (as discussed earlier in this chapter) is related to a competitive mindset. With this mentality, you believe that, in every situation you enter, you must compete with others, as there is only so much of what you want to go around. A scarcity attitude only promotes anxiety and fear because you are fearful that there are not enough resources for everyone.

Become happier and more content in your life by adopting an abundance mentality. To build an abundance mentality habit, you must flip the switch to a plentiful mentality. Accomplish this mindset change in three easy steps:

1. When you find your thoughts entering a scarcity mode, yell "Stop!" (under your breath, of course).

2. Replace your thought with the mantra "The world is plentiful" or "There is an unlimited amount of what I need" or a similar abundance mentality thought.

3. Repeat this until you have dislodged your scarcity thoughts and developed the habit of thinking abundantly. Over time, your new abundance attitude will not only decrease your anxiety but also increase your level of happiness.

CHAPTER 8

THE GIFT

"The great and glorious masterpiece of man is to live with purpose. When we have a purpose, we are not just a collection of pieces but we make up a masterpiece."
— Michel de Montaigne, Renaissance philosopher

I HOPE YOU HAVE BEGUN TO REALIZE THE TRUE ESSENCE OF *FALL UP!* AND DEVELOPING **TRANSCEND-ABILITY.** It is not about tragedy. Rather, the true essence of this book is about giving yourself the "Gift." The introduction mentioned how Michael J. Fox called his Parkinson's a gift because it forced him to make his purpose a verb. He created his foundation, which has made a significant difference helping others cope with this disease. As Michael J. discovered, when you live in purpose, the gift is that your life has become a masterpiece full of joy and contentment.

On the other side of the coin, I discovered the hard truth about not living in purpose and how that can affect your mental health. At the age of twenty-four, I lived on the beautiful Hawaiian Island of Kauai. It is dubbed the Garden Isle for a reason.

Everything is green and gorgeous. Wherever you look, you can see a beautiful waterfall sneaking out from the vegetation. The birds are the most astounding colors—blues, greens, yellows—and when you look into the water, the fish dazzle you with the same magnificence.

My days consisted of going to the beach, surfing, snorkeling, hiking to a new waterfall, and playing golf on a magnificent course adjacent to the coast. At night, I worked as a waiter, and before every shift, I would eat some of the freshest fish on the planet. My life was full of fun and pleasurable experiences.

Kauai is a magnificent and magical place, and I was living in paradise on Earth. Then, I grew bored and very unhappy. My spirit got tired of a life filled with a hedonistic bent. At that moment in time, my authentic self was lost. There was a spiritual void that desperately needed to be filled. I felt a very strong urge to get off the island and find a more meaningful existence.

These deep-rooted feelings at this time in my life enlightened me to this one undeniable truth: **Paradise without purpose is not paradise**.

This Hawaiian experience was my wake-up call to the importance of the "Gift." The true essence of this book is you don't need tragedy to discover your authentic self. But you must give yourself the "Gift"—the gift of living in purpose. It must permeate everything you do. Purpose must be at the center of your world. When this happens, that void of despair and loneliness will dissolve, and your unease and anxiety will diminish. When you give yourself the "Gift," you will move toward a life filled with contentment, happiness, and peace of mind that you so desire. **Living in purpose creates your paradise!**

Purpose must be the center of your world.

Recently, Dr. Martin Seligman, author of *Flourish* and one of the founding fathers of positive psychology, has proposed that we will find contentment and happiness from five distinct avenues, which he labeled PERMA. This newest model is derived from much research as well as former frameworks that he and others have created concerning the cornerstones of happiness and living a fulfilled life. In this model, the *P* stands for **Positive Emotions** such as gratitude, pleasure, inspiration, and hope. Daily positive emotions contributes to our level of happiness. The *E* represents **Engagement** in the happiness equation. Here, when you are truly engaged in a task, you will experience flow and have a sense of peace and fulfillment. The *R* indicates the importance of positive **Relationships** in our lives. Authentic connections with others is the core to our well-being. The *M* represents **Meaning** in our lives. Meaning comes from giving ourselves to others and serving the world. Helping humanity will bring meaning into our lives and a greater sense of well-being. The *A* stands for our **Accomplishments**. When we accomplish a difficult task, we have a greater sense of well-being. Seligman proposed that by adding these five elements into our lives, we will flourish and find the happiness in our lives that we seek.

While Seligman is a giant in the field of psychology, and has contributed immensely to our understanding of well-being, this newest model misses a major note in the song of happiness. In his model, meaning has been separated as a part of happiness. This is an inaccurate picture of having a fulfilled life.

Instead of just one spoke on the wheel of happiness, living in purpose must be the center of the wheel. To have the highest levels of positive emotion, the situation must be meaningful to you. Achievements won't matter to you very much if they have no real purpose to you and your life. Relationships that have the most meaning and purpose to you will lead to the greatest level of happiness. It is unlikely that you will get into flow if the situation has no meaning to you. Thus, your level of happiness, high or low, is driven by your level of meaning and purpose.

Historical Contexts of Meaning

To be fulfilled and happy, living in purpose must weave its cosmic thread throughout your life. But this is nothing new as this human truth has been known for eons. Aristotle advocated for **Eudaimonic** well-being. According to this great philosopher, merely pursuing pleasure was not enough, and, more importantly, it only contributed to a short-lived level of happiness. To Aristotle, our long-term happiness comes when our lives are wrapped within a meaningful existence. Happiness that lasts is a result from doing what is worth doing rather than the pursuit of wine and material goods.

This human truth that has crossed the seas of time is clear— living in purpose is the key ingredient to creating a fulfilled life.

Pain from Not Living in Purpose

What happens when purpose is not at your center? What happens when your life appears devoid of meaning? What happens when you have not made *purpose* a verb?

Television's bard, Rod Serling, who created the Aesop-like series known as *The Twilight Zone*, knew the answer to this essential life question and shared it with us in many episodes. One particular episode, "The Changing of the Guard," opens with Professor Fowler, who has worked for fifty-one years teaching at Rock Springs School, being forced into retirement by the headmaster of the school. Professor Fowler is devastated. Poignantly, he begins to dwell upon his lifework as antiquated drivel. Sadly, he states, "I gave them nothing. Poetry that left their minds the minute they themselves left. Aged slogans that were out of date when I taught them. Quotations dear to me that were meaningless to them. I was a failure—I moved nobody. I motivated nobody. I left no imprint on anybody."

Completely dejected and believing his life is without worth, he takes out his pistol and is about to commit suicide. Just at that moment, he hears the school bells ringing, when there should be silence. Professor Fowler walks to his classroom to investigate the commotion, and there he gets his wake-up call.

Sitting at all the desks are ghosts of some of his now-deceased students. They begin to share how he made a difference in their lives, how they remembered his poems when they were at war, how his words gave them courage, and how his stories gave them hope. His former students all explained how his teaching had enriched their lives beyond measure and time.

This experience transforms Professor Fowler. Believing he made his mark and his teaching had significant value, he finds his tranquility. He now is content to retire. Those students gave him much more than a scholastic lesson—they gave him the best gift that students could give to their teacher—he discovered he left a meaningful imprint upon their lives.

Rod Serling gave us a wake-up call to the essence of the human condition. You must find a meaningful purpose in your actions. When you do, your life will be filled with a euphoria beyond compare. If you do not, you might succumb to your darkest emotions.

Fill Your Bucket with Purpose.

What happens when you don't have students to fill your life with purpose? What happens when you ask yourself if you are living in purpose and the answer is "no"?

When this happens, you will suffer some type of emotional

fallout. Renowned psychologist Carl Jung stated it this way: "Lack of meaning in our lives is our greatest neurosis." Without purpose, negative emotions will permeate your inner being. In turn, you will desperately search for ways to alleviate this psychic pain and fill this void.

Some people try to fill this dark void and reduce the pain with substances and/or risky behaviors. This is where addiction comes into play. Put simply, think of a person addicted to shopping. Now visualize a happiness bucket. Their happiness gets filled when clothes are purchased, but this state is only temporary. This existential vacuum has created holes in the bucket. Thus, you must continue to buy more and more stuff to keep the bucket full. The cycle never ends—thus the addiction to shopping, and the principle to all addictions.

The only way to fill your bucket is to live in purpose.

Besides addiction, some people try to fill this void with endless distraction. Spending countless hours on Facebook, Twitter, or other social media accounts as well as watching mindless television distracts you from facing the psychic void of not living a life filled with purpose. But this distraction is only temporary. Eventually you will need to answer this eternal question.

The only way to fill your bucket is to live in purpose.

Another way to try to fill this void is through changing your situation. The epitome of the "midlife crisis" is when someone buys a fancy sports car, has an extramarital affair, or gets divorced. This person believes that completely changing their life will alleviate this psychic pain and fill this dark void. Changing your life does not change you. Your unhappiness will follow you wherever you go.

The only way to fill your bucket is to live in purpose.

Purpose unlocks your super-power.

What happens when you ask yourself if you are living in purpose and the answer is yes? What happens when purpose is the center of the hub of your life?

Making *purpose* a verb is your super-power. It unleashes your talents and will raise your game to another level. I feel this power every time I take the stage to make a presentation. Because I am a professional speaker, most people think I am extroverted and thrive on being the center of attention. But nothing can be further from the truth. I am much more introverted and prefer a dim light compared to the spotlight. But when I speak at conferences, sometimes to two thousand people, I become much more gregarious and super-extroverted. I know my words will make a difference for many people in the audience. I am living in purpose when I speak, and this makes me want to be entertaining, enlightening, and connect with my audience. Living in purpose empowers me on stage to become the person I want to be—the person I am meant to be.

If you look in history books, you will see this human truth throughout the pages of time. Living in purpose supercharges commitment and courage, gives you peace of mind, and provides you with supreme confidence. You will have a supreme level of mental and emotional toughness when you live in purpose.

Purpose increases courage and confidence.

One historical tale that most know well involves the bicycle-making brothers from Dayton, Ohio. What is lesser known is how purpose supercharged their commitment and courage so that they could change the world.

As history is written, these brothers were in one of the first amazing races. But it was not a bicycle race; rather, it was a race to build the first flying machine. Actually, at the beginning of the twentieth century, there was a worldwide race to invent the first reliable flying machine. Countries had created teams with their best engineers along with immense funding to win this essential race.

These two brothers, Orville and Wilbur Wright, had neither a formal education in engineering nor much money to fund such a project. In fact, they used all their money from their bicycle works to fund their inventions. To make matters worse, the press thought these brothers were a couple of quacks. Even their local townspeople believed these brothers were a bit strange in their behavior.

But none of this mattered because these brothers were supremely confident and committed to their path. But it wasn't easy. Failure after failure pervaded their journey. Finally, they flew their Wright Flyer for eighteen seconds at Kitty Hawk, North Carolina, in 1903.

Most people believe this to be the moment in time that the Wright Brothers had won the aviation race. But this was actually just the start of the real race. The Wright Brothers knew that eighteen seconds was not enough to win the aviation race and change the future of flying. They had to keep their Wright Flyer in the air for much longer.

It took five more years that included many near-fatal crashes. In fact, Orville crashed so badly during one of their flying experiments that he was rendered physically unable to ever fly again. But the brothers kept going and eventually found their destiny. In 1908, Wilbur flew his flyer for almost one hour in France during a flying exhibition. Now the world took notice and the birth of aviation began.

When asked why he was so confident that he could win the aviation race with all the odds stacked against him, Wilbur Wright answered in simple, but prophetic, terms. Wilbur did not persist in the face of danger on a daily basis because he loved to fly or because he was passionate about flying. He simply said he wanted to **"teach the world how to fly."**

Wilbur and Orville Wright became icons in our history books because purpose gave them wings of confidence. Nothing would stop these brothers in their quest. Their actions were lifted by the heights of purpose. They made their purpose a verb, and it changed their lives as much as it changed ours.

Purpose promotes supreme commitment.

Living in purpose will also give you supreme commitment toward a goal. Philippe Petit, who was featured in the Academy Award-winning documentary *Man on Wire* is an amazing example of this human truth. While just a young boy, Philippe saw a picture of the Twin Towers of the World Trade Center in New York City, and at that moment decided he would walk across them on a tight wire. Yes, it was a crazy thought and a dangerous one. But for the next twenty years, Philippe dedicated his life to mastering his craft and fulfilling his dream.

When he got older, he visited New York City three times to develop a plan on how he could get to the top of the towers and set the stage for his death-defying feat. It was trespassing, so he needed to be stealth and craft a plan that would work. On his third visit, he brought his team with him and they decided to shoot arrows across from one tower to the other. These arrows were tied to a rope and then they would pull them tight enough so Philippe could walk across.

Then he did the unthinkable. He walked across the towers on a tight wire, and people on the streets of New York City were transfixed. Thousands stopped to watch. The police wanted to arrest him, while the media made him an instant celebrity.

When he came off his wire and touched the ground once more, he was asked this simple question, "Why did you do it?" Philippe poignantly answered, "There is no why."

He did not do this extremely risky feat for praise, accolades, fame, or fortune. He did it because Philippe saw this daring event as his purpose and he took action. Because he lived in purpose all those years, Philippe was completely committed and confident he would accomplish this most dangerous act. When he made *purpose* a verb, he had premier emotional toughness and achieved his dreams.

Purpose sparks the flame of inspiration.

Victor Frankl stated that striving to live in purpose is your primary motivational force. When you live in purpose, you will live an inspired life full of vitality, enthusiasm, and passion. Living in purpose gives you the inspiration to thrive and flourish.

Just look around. Find people who are truly inspired. Ask them why. You will discover that they feel aligned with their purpose and authentic self—whatever that might be for them. And it does not matter what they do or who they are. They might be the janitor at your office, a gardener, or the teacher at your children's school. But each will tell you that they live a life worth living.

Nothing can stop a person who is living in purpose. They act as if they have a burning flame of inspiration, and nothing can snuff it out. Take the wonderful example of Eleanor Roosevelt. She led an inspired life with endless energy to make a difference. She was the first presidential spouse to hold a multitude of press conferences, write thousands of newspaper articles, and speak many times at national conventions. She was nonstop in her desire to make a difference in the lives of others.

Her main message was to boost as well as reinforce the rights of the less advantaged. Eleanor consistently addressed as well as fought for gender equality in American life. She hosted and sponsored many national meetings that focused on the needs of women such as the White House Conference on the Emergency Needs of Unemployed Women and the White House Conference on Camps for Unemployed Women.

Eleanor also promoted the equality of all races. She became the first white resident of Washington, DC to join the local chapters of both the NAACP and National Urban League. She also attended and addressed the annual conventions of both organizations. She successfully backed an effort to create the Justice Department's Civil Rights Division, and worked as a board member of the NAACP, among other civil rights organizations.

In addition, Eleanor championed the rights of the poor. As an example, she launched an experimental community in Arthurdale, West Virginia, for the families of unemployed coal miners. The idea was to create a self-sufficient community with the intention that they could combine subsistence farming with simple industries to reclaim their economic footing.

Following Franklin Roosevelt's death, her role in human rights grew to international proportions. Eleanor Roosevelt pressed the US to join and support the United Nations, and she became one of its first delegates. She served as the first chair of the UN Commission on Human Rights and helped draft the Universal Declaration of Human Rights. She believed this to be the Magna Carta of human rights and a way to protect the endowed rights of everyone in the world.

Eleanor Roosevelt is one of the most beloved icons in our history. She lived in purpose, and this sparked a vibrant life worth living. Interestingly, famed historian Doris Kearns Goodwin claimed that Eleanor's flame only blew out much later in life when she saw herself as useless and her actions meaningless.

Finding purpose is a choice.

Our life is a product of our choices. You can choose to live a life full of selfishness and ego-serving activities. You can choose an endless pursuit of materials and believe they will lead to your happiness. You can choose an "us" vs. "them" mentality and focus all your energy on the "me" in that equation. You can choose to be fearful of the criticism of others because you don't live up to their standards. You can choose to believe that you will never find your Lifesong or sweet spot in life.

Or you can choose an inspired life by living in purpose. You can choose to see your hardships as blessings. You can choose to believe in the power of service. You have the choice to harmonize with your Lifesong. You can choose to fall up and therefore develop transcend-ability. You have this freedom to choose.

When you make the right choice, you will lead the life you only imagined. This is the secret! You don't need a tragedy to find it. This is your wake-up call!

But do more than choose an inspired life—take action. Einstein said that nothing happens until something moves. *Happiness* is a verb. *Inspiration* is a verb. *Purpose* is a verb. As Ohna told us in the parable, "Be the love you seek." Ohna wants you to "be" and take action toward creating your life into a masterpiece.

The following are action steps to help you take action and "be" the person you were meant to be:

Live in purpose every day.

One of famed musician Stephen Stills's best-known lyrics is: "If you can't be with the one you love, honey, love the one you're with." Stills's lyrics are timeless wisdom. Your first priority is to align your life path and career with your Lifesong (as discussed in a previous chapter). When you do this, you have found your calling. In this case, you might never want to retire because, as Joseph Campbell told us, you are following your bliss.

Unfortunately, many people are stuck in their current job, and they just can't afford to change their life and move into an entirely new career path, regardless if it is for the best. Perhaps you have a mortgage and three children in college, and leaving your current career is not a realistic option. In this case, do what Stephen Stills tells us and "Love the one you're with." You can retune your job and life so it realigns with your Lifesong—so that you make *purpose* a verb every day. This process involves following four fundamental steps:

Step 1: Tune into your Lifesong.

First, recall that special moment in your life in which you felt purposeful and had a meaningful impact upon others and/or the world. It is a moment in time that stands out from all the rest because it lifted your spirit to another place and time. Everyone has experienced that moment. Venue is irrelevant as this inspirational moment could have happened at work, at school, during a sport competition, or in a life-or-death situation.

Here is a wonderful example of this process. (Please note that for this particular story, the names and places have been changed to protect confidentiality and security):

Bill London was not always a financial advisor. In his former life, he was Lt. Bill London, an army medic in Afghanistan.

Lieutenant Bill explained that his most inspirational experience came when he saved the life of Private Williams. The private's squad had been on a routine surveillance of a small village when they all got pinned down in an abandoned house by enemy fire. Private Williams was the designated lookout, so he waited behind. When he saw his squad in dire trouble, he got into his Humvee and rode into the village with bullets swarming all around him. Private Williams bashed the Humvee into one of the walls of the house, his squad jumped in, and he drove them all to safety.

"Unfortunately, Private Williams was shot five times during this exploit," Lieutenant Bill explained, and then added, "He was airlifted to my makeshift medical center, near Kabul. This kid had a 5 percent chance of living. He lost enough blood for two people, but I was not going to leave him. A kid with this much courage and heart was going to get everything I had, so I stood over him for five long hours. He then fell into a coma for two weeks. Whether it was an angel on his shoulder or just pure luck, I don't know, but Private Williams awoke and then gave me a thumbs up. I knew then he would be okay."

Lieutenant Bill said that this moment in time was his most inspirational experience.

For the first step, list a moment in your life that gave you immense inspiration when you had a meaningful impact on another person or in a situation. Make it just one or two paragraphs.

_____

_____

_____

_____

_____

_____

_____

_____

_____

Step 2: Discover the "why" of your Lifesong.

Once you have discovered your Lifesong moment, then you must understand why that moment was so inspirational to you. "Why" is the cornerstone to this step.

For Lieutenant Bill, he explained to me that his "why" was that he was "saving lives" in the army and this was extremely inspirational.

For you, discover the "why" of your inspirational moment. The "why" leads to the next step.

Step 3: Create the notes to your Lifesong.

The notes of your Lifesong are primers. According to psychologists, primers are powerful stimuli such as words, actions, and images that push your emotions in one direction or another. Music is also a primer and everyone can relate to how a song can make you happy or extremely sad. The same principle applies to the right word, image, or action. These notes (or primers) must be aligned with the _why_ factor of your inspirational moment.

For Lieutenant Bill, the why of his inspirational moment became his motif and the crux of his primers. Therefore, Lieutenant Bill's buzz phrase is "saving lives." For his image, Lieutenant Bill was fortunate that a fellow medic took his picture while he was saving the life of Private Williams, and now uses this image for his wallpaper picture on his iPhone. Lieutenant Bill's action was a thumbs-up because that reminds him of the moment Private Williams awoke from his coma.

To complete this step, you need to discover buzzwords, images, and actions that capture the emotions you had during your amazing moment. It is difficult to get all three, but get at least one primer for this process, and then you can proceed to the final step in this process.

Step 4: Create the Lifesong habit.

Routines build habits. The notes developed in the previous step lend themselves beautifully into a routine that can be used throughout the day to prompt the emotions of your inspirational state, causing you to tune into your Lifesong whenever necessary.

For Lieutenant Bill, being a financial advisor is draining. Clients are demanding. The market is like a bad roller coaster ride, with no stabilization in sight. It is difficult for anyone to stay inspired every day. But Lieutenant Bill exhibits positive powerful emotions, regardless of the situation, because he uses his buzzwords, image, and action whenever he needs a positive emotional lift in his day. Tuning into his Lifesong has become a powerful positive habit of success for Lieutenant Bill.

Like Lieutenant Bill, use your buzzwords, image, and action throughout the day. Based upon this process, you will be able to live in your purpose on a daily basis, regardless of situation or circumstance.

CHAPTER 9

CREATE A CULTURE
OF TRANSCEND-ABILITY

"Every time I have made a decision that
is best for the planet, I have made money.
Our customers know that—and they want to be
part of that environmental commitment."
— Yvon Chouinard, founder and CEO of Patagonia

THE PRINCIPLE OF TRANSCEND-ABILITY EXTENDS FAR BEYOND THE LEVEL OF AN INDIVIDUAL. Achieving transcendence can occur at the organizational level. More importantly, effective leaders can help corporations, organizations, and teams evolve through the stages of transcendence and find their sweet spot. When this occurs, both the company as well as the community benefit immensely. It all depends upon the leadership and their vision. This chapter illustrates the benefits from creating a culture of transcend-ability.

Countries benefit from a culture of transcend-ability.

When former South African President Nelson Mandela created a culture of transcend-ability, he transformed his country into a better place to live. Much has been written about the struggles of Nelson Mandela to end the apartheid system in his country using "Ghandi"-like means. But Mandela was not always the peaceful warrior. In 1964, he was sentenced to life imprisonment for plotting to overthrow the government through hundreds of acts of violent sabotage. His twenty-seven years of imprisonment, most in the harsh environment of Robben Island, were unbearably cruel. Not only was he confined to a small cell, with a bucket for a toilet, and forced to hard labor in a quarry, he could only receive one visitor every six months for thirty minutes.

However, these harsh and bitter experiences did not harden his heart, but rather awakened him to his life's purpose. Nelson Mandela exemplifies the message Ohna was telling us in the parable—"Be the love you seek." Mandela let go of any personal animosity and showered his oppressors with love instead of hate. He did not dwell on the past; instead, he focused only on how to help his country. His being was engulfed with making the world a better place for his children and his children's children, and so on. Because Mandela possessed the highest level of transcend-ability and created a culture to reflect this principle, his country has healed greatly from the wounds of apartheid and racism.

Business benefits from a culture of transcend-ability.

Another great leadership story that involved creating a culture of transcend-ability started in Chalumna, a small African village by a river. In this village, blindness had become associated with growing old. The saying in the village was that before you had white hair, it was normal to be blind. More than 90 percent of the villagers in this area would lose their sight—blindness had become a way of life.

The culprit to the disease of river blindness is a tiny black fly.

It bites the person at the river and leaves larvae behind in the person's bloodstream. The parasitic worms rapidly multiply and spread throughout the body. Amazingly and chillingly, the parasitic worms can grow up to two feet and live for fourteen years inside the human host. They spread throughout the skin and upward to the ocular nerve. Not only does this cause severe itching, but also can make the person blind.

Unfortunately, this tragedy was not confined to this small village. According to the World Health Organization, in the 1970s, 85 million people were at risk of river blindness. Not only was river blindness present in Africa, the disease had spread to Latin America as well as many other undeveloped areas that use the river for their water supply.

As time went by, this problem began to take on epic proportions. More than a million people had suffered from river blindness. Disease-control scientists knew they must try to eradicate this scourge. Some drugs had been created to mollify this disease, but the side effects, in some cases, were deadly. In addition, insect control did not work as the flies were too prolific and could spawn too rapidly. Pesticides were also not very effective. The ability to effectively control this parasite and disease had come to a dead end. Then by chance, one of the nation's leading pharmaceutical firms, Merck, discovered a drug that could eradicate a strain of horse worms. They realized that this drug might be the secret weapon to wipe out river blindness from the face of the earth. More importantly, the side effects were extremely small to nil.

The CEO of Merck, Ray Vagelos, was awakened to the plight of these villagers and knew he had to make a fateful decision for the company. Testing, manufacturing, and distributing a drug for human consumption is a vast undertaking. It usually takes a decade and upwards of $100 million to bring a drug to the marketplace.

Another issue was that the drug was designed to get rid of worms in horses, and it was unknown if it would work with cross species (humans). Also, if there were side effects with humans, then this could damage the marketability of the drug to horses. If the drug did not work in people, then some might think it would not work with horses as well. This was a big risk.

The biggest dilemma, however, was that this drug had no commercial value for humans. The people who needed the drug could not afford it. Furthermore, no international organization, private foundation, or nation wanted to contribute financially to help bring this drug to market. Undoubtedly, this drug would be a loser economically.

How can you develop a drug that is not profitable but will better mankind? This has been an eternal question for many pharmaceutical companies. Leaders with transcend-ability know the answer. Vagelos knew the answer.

Vagelos is a leader who understands the importance of a company's service to the world. He believed that medicine is for the people and that profits must follow from that creed. Vagelos knew that Merck had the strength as a company to take this drug to market, even if this drug was going to be an economic loser.

Vagelos decided that Merck would commit to developing this drug. The company's stockholders were against him. Business experts believed he was making an incredible blunder. But Ray Vagelos knew his company must serve mankind—first and foremost.

The drug, Mectizan, was developed and then distributed to the people in need. It became the miracle drug for river blindness. Villagers would walk all night across many miles so that they could take it. Mectizan virtually eradicated this scourge from the world. The World Health Organization stated that this was one of the greatest medical achievements of mankind.

Mectizan and its benefits for the world created a culture of transcend-ability, which permeated the foundation at Merck. As such, the company erected a statue called "The gift of sight." This statue shows a boy walking in front of a blind old man. Both the boy and blind man are holding a cane with the cane acting as a guide for the old man. This statue was representative of a scene far too prevalent before the drug was developed. The statue sits in front of Merck headquarters in New Jersey for all to see. When Merck employees view it, a sense of pride is inevitable, and this powerful emotion will sweeten any journey that a Merck employee will make.

In addition, while the development of Mectizan was not profitable to Merck's bottom line in the short term, this experience had positive ramifications for years to come. The development of Mectizan showed that Merck was a company with integrity that does the right thing for the world. This social consciousness mantra helped to bring the best research talent to the company. In turn, the best and brightest have created great discoveries for Merck, which will increase their profits in the future. Giving away the drug and serving the common good created a momentous ripple effect that will extend for decades.

Patagonia, the famed outdoor clothing company, created a culture of transcend-ability by serving another needy source, our environment. Patagonia's founder, Yvon Chouinard, followed the mantra "Be the love you seek" for his beloved environment, and in turn, created a very profitable company. The story begins when the young Yvon fell in love with mountain climbing. His love for mountain climbing prompted him to start his first company that made gear to help individuals traverse any mountain. From there, he extended his company's products and began to make mountain-climbing clothing.

To build Patagonia, Yvon had to travel across the globe looking for new products, new markets, and new materials for his new company. While on business trips, he would also look for new surf spots and mountains to climb. These experiences were extremely painful to his heart as he saw firsthand the devastation to the environment caused by big business in search of the bottom line. As Yvon stated, "I saw that human beings and the natural world were on a collision course."

Human activities were inflicting harsh and irreversible damage to the environment and its critical resources. He saw that essential forests and grasslands were disappearing across Europe. In Russia, he saw how they had devastated their land and contaminated their cities by keeping up with the West. Yvon saw how fast food companies were destroying the rainforest by clearing it to graze cattle. Closer to home, in Wyoming, he saw the fish population receding in great numbers because of the toxicity of the groundwater. Such experiences moved Yvon to become much more than just a businessman in search of profits.

His **wake-up call** came in his backyard in Ventura, California. Urban development was about to ruin a beautiful estuary where birds lived, muskrats swam, and eels spawned. Yvon saw how one person, Mark Capelli, could make a difference with a powerful message. Mark presented a slide show at a council meeting showing that this estuary was teeming with wild life, and Mark stopped the project. This experience **flipped the switch** for Yvon, and he decided that Patagonia needs to be a protective steward for our environment—this became Patagonia's **Lifesong**.

Patagonia has created a variety of company initiatives to support their Lifesong. As an example, every year the company holds a tools-for-grassroots conference about protecting our environment, which helps people learn how to start their own similar campaign. Most impressively, the company gives 1 percent of sales of pretax profits to assist grass-roots campaigns that are helping our environment. To date, Patagonia has given away more than $22 million to protect our environment. Additionally, Patagonia will match funds given for donations by their employees to their favorite environmental causes. It also gives $2,000 to each of their employees to go toward a hybrid/electric car purchase.

Furthermore, Patagonia's company mantra is to reduce, repair, reuse, and recycle. Patagonia uses recycled paper for their catalog. They use cotton that was organically grown and dyes for their products that will not pollute the environment. Also, they have a companywide recycling center, where employees can bring their home goods for recycling.

Equally important, Yvon believes he has a responsibility to influence other companies to follow suit and be environmentally protective. Because of this philosophy, Yvon created the 1% for the Planet movement in 2001. This charity pushes businesses to give away at least 1 percent of their net annual sales to groups on a list of researched and approved environmental organizations. The intent is to fund many diverse environmental groups so collectively they will be more powerful and help save our environment from devastation. Yvon wants the Lifesong of Patagonia to be heard throughout the business world.

All this doing good for the environment does good for business. Patagonia is consistently voted one of the top one hundred companies to work for, with very high retention and low absenteeism. Also, Yvon has mentioned that consumers know the pro-environmental purpose of Patagonia, which promotes a substantial increase in the purchase of their products, year after year.

The ultimate goal for Patagonia is to stay in business for at least another hundred years, so that they can be our environment's big brother. Patagonia has made a great start.

Teams benefit from a culture of transcend-ability.

The benefits of a service mantra and in creating a culture of transcend-ability is not only for corporations. This principle can have immense benefits to teams as well. John Wooden is the prototypical leader who created a culture of transcend-ability for his basketball team. His leadership style focused on serving his players first, and, in turn, they rose to an amazing level of excellence.

Wooden learned many of his lessons from his upbringing on his family farm in southern Indiana. His father taught him key life lessons growing up as a farmer. First, never think you are better than someone else. Second, always learn from your mistakes. Third, focus on what you can control and forget what you can't. Fourth, value your integrity. Finally, make sure you give back to the community.

Wooden took those life lessons to heart when he coached at UCLA. The foundation for Wooden's philosophy starts with one of his greatest contributions to the genre: the Pyramid of Success. The Pyramid of Success is a compilation of building blocks that comprise his leadership philosophy that guided his communication style, his attitude, how he ran practices, and how he coached during games. The Pyramid of Success was the basis for creating a culture of transcend-ability on the UCLA hardwood.

While there are many gems in his Pyramid of Success, three stand out for building a team culture of transcendence: integrity, cooperation, and team spirit. Wooden believed integrity is a purity of intention from which all your actions and words emanate. Cooperation implied believing in the inherent interest in others, and the best way to winning includes incorporating as many players as possible into the mix. To Wooden, team spirit implied an ego-less attitude in which you must sacrifice personal interests for the betterment of the team.

While his Pyramid of Success helped to create one of the greatest success stories in college basketball history, it was also aclear window into John Wooden's heart as a leader. His true purpose was to be a leader of service. In his retirement, he would rarely discuss his winning seasons; rather, his joy came from how his boys turned into men of service and how they impacted the world. He relished that so many of his players had become attorneys, doctors, teachers, and other service professionals. This is John Wooden's true **Lifesong**.

In turn, Wooden's Lifesong was heard by all his players. His players knew of their leader's true intentions and how much he sincerely cared about them. Bill Walton, one of his players as well as one of the greatest basketball players of all time, mentioned how much John Wooden meant to him as a mentor and role model as a person. He stated that Wooden made him the man that he is today: one who cares about the world and others.

Like Walton, so many of Wooden's players knew that their coach cared about their personal development. They knew that winning was secondary; becoming a better human being was the ultimate purpose of his coaching. Because of this transcend-ability leadership style, his players were hyper-motivated to perform for Wooden. They trusted his words and strategies; and, in culmination, he became a coach without peer. As the men's head basketball coach at UCLA, John Wooden won ten NCAA championships.

Great leaders such as Nelson Mandela, Ray Vagelos, Yvon Chouinard, and John Wooden have created a culture of transcend-ability that led to having a meaningful impact in their respective fields as well as in their communities. The following are three key steps to help you become a leader who promotes a culture of transcend-ability:

Step 1: Build your pyramid of success.

135

The first step in creating the culture you desire at your organization is to develop a strong vision. Your vision will allow you to communicate clearly and consistently, which in turn creates a strong culture.

However, developing a vision that is aligned with your strengths and values can be difficult. A method to best capture your vision is to create a pyramid of success. John Wooden stated many times that his great success stemmed from his Pyramid of Success. You can google an image of his Pyramid of Success, but in a nutshell his pyramid is a series of fifteen blocks, with each block representing a different quality of success. For instance, the bottom tier includes the qualities of industriousness, friendship, loyalty, cooperation, and enthusiasm. Some of his middle blocks include self-control and taking initiative, and the top block represents competitive greatness. These blocks helped Wooden to communicate his vision consistently during practice and in games, which promoted a championship culture at UCLA.

Your first step to developing a culture of transcend-ability is to create your own pyramid of success in which you name fifteen blocks that represent different qualities. As an example, these could include integrity, honesty, or service.

Ultimately, you must choose the blocks that best represent a culture of transcend-ability that you want to develop in your organization. Write all fifteen blocks in the spaces that follow:

———————————————————

———————————————————

———————————————————

_____

_____

_____

_____

_____

_____

_____

_____

_____

_____

_____

Step 2: Create a vision tagline.

Steve Jobs wanted Apple to make a "dent in the universe." This was his tagline for Apple, which led to a cultural revolution in personal computers as well as in the music and phone industry. Making a dent in the universe implied that Apple would change the world in a positive way—and it definitely has!

Once you have created your pyramid with its blocks, then it

will be much easier to create a vision tagline related to transcend-ability. As an example, Yvon Chouinard's vision tagline would be "We are servants of the environment," because his company is set up to protect and defend our environment. John Wooden's vision tagline would be "From boys to men," because he was very concerned with helping his players become men of character.

Now create your vision tagline in one sentence. Write it below:

_____

Step 3: Create a culture of transcend-ability.

Once you have your pyramid of success and your vision tagline, now you can create a powerful culture in your organization. Look to your pyramid and tagline as a way to communicate clearly. Adhering to the building blocks in your pyramid will make your message resonate on a consistent basis. When you are consistent and clear in your message, your staff will view you as more authentic, leading to greater influence. Also, your pyramid should be your guide as how you motivate your staff as well as yourself. The pyramid will focus your intentions, which in turn will inspire those around you.

Once you have achieved a clear and succinct vision, a culture of transcend-ability can be created in your organization. This should not only increase profits but also promote a positive impact upon the community.

EPILOGUE

"When you are inspired by some great purpose,
some extraordinary project,
all of your thoughts break their bonds:
Your mind transcends limitations,
your consciousness expands in every direction,
and you find yourself in a new, great, and wonderful world.
Dormant forces, faculties, and talents come alive,
and you discover yourself to be a greater person by far
than you ever dreamed yourself to be."

— Patanjali (Ancient philosopher,
written more than two thousand years ago)

THESE WORDS OF PATANJALI HAVE CROSSED THE SEAS OF TIME, YET THEY SPEAK THE TRUTH TODAY AS THEY DID IN HIS DAY. You are the extraordinary project when you fill your life with purpose. Living your purpose makes you transcend your limitations, your dormant forces and talents will come alive, and you will discover yourself to be a far better person than you ever dreamt to be. This is not an ancient truth or a modern truth. This is our truth.

I leave you with these simple words of eternal wisdom on your way to happiness and success:

Find your purpose.

Create your path.

Make the commitment.

Enjoy the journey.

Be the love you seek!

YOUR FALL UP STORY

Many of you who are reading this book have an amazing story about how you turned your tragedy into transcendence and achieved transcend-ability. I would love to hear from you and to hear about your own story. Please contact me at mentalrules24@msn.com or visit www.drgreggsteinberg.com and send me a message. You can also share your story on the Fall Up Facebook group page.

ACKNOWLEDGMENTS

I WOULD LIKE TO THANK ALL THE WONDERFUL PEOPLE WHO HAVE MADE THIS BOOK POSSIBLE. First, I would like to thank all those who allowed me to use their stories for this book, and, from their stories, helped me develop the concept of transcend-ability. Their stories have changed my thinking and enlightened me to a whole new world of transcendence.

I would also like to thank Joel Bunkowske, who sat with me at Starbucks for many hours and discussed how people can turn their tragedy into transcendence. I would also like to thank my editors, Mike Towle and Bea Julia, who helped make this book better. Also, I am appreciative that People Shine Publishing helped turned this book into a reality.

RESOURCES

Chapter 1: Introduction: The New Science of Super-Resilience

Buckingham, Marcus. *Go Put Your Strengths to Work*. New York: Free Press, 2010.

Bulayskaya, Valery. "Life Story of Czech Supermodel Petra Nemcova." *Youth Time Magazine*, June 6, 2014.

Dweck, Carol. *Mindset*. New York: Ballantine Books, 2007.

Fox, Michael J. *Lucky Man: A Memoir*. New York: Hachette Books, 2003)

"Importance of Fire to a Forest, The." http://www.fresh-fromflorida.com/Divisions-Offices/Florida-Forest-Service/Wildland-Fire/Prescribed-Fire/The-Natural-Role-of-Fire, viewed 2018.

Kielburger, Craig, and Mark Kielburger. *Me to We*. New York: Touchstone Books, 2008.

Kübler-Ross, Elisabeth, and David Kessler. *On Grief and Grieving*. New York: Scribner, 2010.

Kushner, Harold. *When All You Ever Wanted Isn't Enough.* New York: Touchstone Books, 2002.

Maslow, Abraham. *A Theory of Motivation.* New York: Martino Fine Books, 2013.

Seligman, Martin. *Learned Optimism.* New York: Vintage, 2006.

Tedeschi, Richard, and Bret Moore. *Transformed by Trauma.* Independent Publishing, 2020.

"Thomas Edison: The Story of Light." *How We Got Here* series, History Channel, viewed in 2017.

Chapter 3: The Wake-up Call

Goleman, Daniel. *Emotional Intelligence.* New York: Bantam Books, 2005.

"Morse Code Connects Us All." *How We Got Here* series. History Channel, viewed in 2015.

Roosevelt, Theodore. *The Strenuous Life.* New York: The Century Company, 1902.

Steinberg, Gregg. *MentalRules for Golf.* Nashville: TowleHouse Publishing, 2003.

Williams, Ted. *My Turn at Bat.* New York: Simon and Schuster, 1969.

Chapter 4: Flip the Switch

Belic, Roko. *Happy Documentary,* 2011.

Dweck, Carol. *Mindset.* New York: Ballantine Books, 2007.

Frankl, Victor. *Man's Search for Meaning.* Washington Square Press, 1997.

Steinberg, Gregg. *Flying Lessons.* Nashville: Thomas Nelson, 2007.

Steinberg, Gregg. "Do You Value Constructive Criticism? Good Thing Harper Lee Did." *The Tennessean*, February 28, 2016.

Steinberg, Gregg. *MentalRules for Golf*. Nashville: Towle-house Publishing, 2003.

Walker, Joseph. "Fake Knee Surgery as Good as Real Procedure." http://www.wsj.com/articles/SB10001424052702304244 904579278442014913458., viewed in 2013.

Chapter 5: Release Your Genius

APSU All Star, Winter edition, 2014.

"Einstein." History Channel, viewed in 2018.

"From Prison Cells to Egg Shells." *Sunday Morning*, viewed in 2015.

"Matisse: The Cutouts." *Sunday Morning*, viewed in 2015.

"Roosevelts: An Intimate History, The." PBS documentary, viewed in 2018.

Steinberg, Gregg. *MentalRules for Golf*. Nashville: Towle-house Publishing, 2003.

"Steve Jobs: Stanford Commencement Speech," https://www.youtube.com/watch?v=UF8uR6Z6KLc, viewed in 2010.

Chapter 6: Discover Your Lifesong

Berra, Yogi. *The Yogi Book*. New York: Workman Publishing, 1999.

Campbell, J., and B. Moyers. *The Power of Myth*. New York: Anchor Publishing, 1991.

"Donny Anderson Story, The." *Sunday Morning*. May 2014.

Terry Fox,
https://www.youtube.com/watch?v=xjgTlCTluPA,
viewed in 2011.

Steinberg, Gregg. *Full Throttle*. New York: John Wiley &
Sons, 2009.

Chapter 7: Make *Purpose* a Verb

Cacioppo, John. *Loneliness: Human Nature and the Need
for Social Connection*. New York: W. W. Norton and
Company, 2008.

"From Amazon to Garden State." *Sunday Morning*, viewed
in 2015.

"Greeks, The." PBS special, viewed in 2018.

"I Can See Clearly Now." PBS special, viewed in 2016.

Kielburger, Craig, and Mark Kielburger. *Me to We*. New
York: Touchtone Books, 2008.

Lyubomirsky, Sonia. *The How of Happiness*. New York:
Penguin, 2007.

Marut, Lama. *Be Nobody*. New York: Atria Books, 2014.

"Rent a Family for the Holidays." *Sunday Morning*, viewed
in 2013.

Steinberg, Gregg. *Flying Lessons*. Nashville: Thomas Nelson,
2007.

Steinberg, Gregg. *Full Throttle*. New York: John Wiley &
Sons, 2009.

Chapter 8. The Gift

Marsh, James. *Man on Wire*. Documentary, 2008.

McCullough, David. *The Wright Brothers*. New York: Simon & Schuster, 2016.

"Roosevelts: An Intimate History, The." PBS documentary, viewed in 2018.

Seligman, Martin. *Flourish*. New York: Atria Books, 2012.

Steinberg, Gregg. *Flying Lessons*. Nashville: Thomas Nelson, 2007.

Chapter 9. Create a Culture of Transcend-ability

Chouinard, Yvon. *Let My People Go Surfing*. New York: Penguin, 2006.

Eknath, Easwaran. *Ghandi the Man*. Nilgiri Press, 2009.

Isaacson, Walter. *Steve Jobs*. New York: Simon & Schuster, 2015.

John Wooden TED talk. https://www.youtube.com/watch?v=0MM-psvqiG8, viewed in 2016.

Useem, Michael. *The Leadership Moment*. New York: Crown, 1999.

THE AUTHOR

D R. GREGG STEINBERG IS A PROFESSOR OF HUMAN PERFORMANCE at Austin Peay State University, near Nashville, Tennessee. *Golf Digest* ranked him one of the world's greatest sports psychologists. He is the author of three mental-toughness books, including the *Washington Post* bestseller *Full Throttle*, which illustrates performance psychology principles applied to business; *Flying Lessons*, which illustrates how to build mental and emotional toughness in children; and *MentalRules for Golf*, which is a golf psychology book. Dr. Steinberg's work has appeared in the *New York Times*, *USA Today*, and the *Wall Street Journal*. He has appeared on numerous television shows, including *Dancing with the Stars* to discuss mental toughness, and he was the sport psychology expert for Fox News during the 2008 Summer Olympics. Dr. Steinberg has also given a TEDx talk called "Fall Up," which explains how to become super-resilient. He lives in Nashville, Tennessee, with his wife Tommie, their son Myles, and their Italian greyhound, Bohdi.